Take a Buttock of Beefe

Verity Isitt

Take a Buttock of Beefe

Verity Isitt

Ashford Press Publishing
Southampton
1987

Published by Ashford Press Publishing 1987
1 Church Road
Shedfield
Hampshire SO3 2HW

British Library Cataloguing in Publication Data
Isitt, Verity
Take a buttock of beefe.
1. Cookery, English — History — 17th century
I. Title
641.5942   TX717

ISBN 0-907069-57-6

Designed and typeset by Jordan and Jordan, Fareham, Hampshire
Printed by Robert Hartnoll (1985) Ltd, Bodmin, Cornwall

For my daughter Helen

Thanks for Help

Mr M. Corbett

Mr and Mrs R. Culverwell

Miss Gena Davies

Mr T. Gadsby

Mr C. Greensit

Mrs G. Howard

Mrs M. Jackaman

Miss B. Millard

Mr and Mrs Christopher Morris

Miss E. Ralph

Mr P. Jeevar

Mr M. Brailsford

Mr P. Jeevar

Mr M. Brailsford

My thanks are to my family and friends for their help and support. They have tried my recipes and given critical approval.

The author and publisher wish to thank the following for kind permission to reproduce black and white pictures:

Rev. P. Angwin (p 127), Bath City Museum (p 54), Bodleian Library Oxford (pp 9, 104, 148, 150, 152, 177), Brecon Museum (pp 26, 37, 39, 61, 64, 81, 87, 170), Fitzwilliam Library, Cambridge (pp 4, 11, 33, 43, 66, 69, 71, 72, 89, 94, 108, 111, 123, 134, 147, 155, 156, 164, 167), Rev. R. Hare (p 97), Harvey's Wine Museum, Bristol (pp 61, 66, 169, 171), Hulton Picture Library (pp 82, 106, 117, 119, 139, 141, 143, 144, 145), Peter Jeevar (pp 49, 51), Magdalene College, Cambridge (pp 14, 40, 73, 76, 113), Museum of London (pp 159, 160, 161), National Portrait Gallery, London (pp 28, 53, 87), National Trust (pp 90, 135), Miss E. Ralph (p 125), Sion Hill Hall Museum and North Yorks police (p 63), Mrs Verey (p 99), Victoria and Albert Museum, London (pp 74, 115, 163), Dean and Chapter of Wells Cathedral (p 121), Welsh Folk Museum (pp 35, 45, 78, 93, 155).

Contents

This dish is too good for any but anglers.

                       Izaak Walton

Well on, brave boyes to your Lord's hearth glittering with fire; where for your mirth Ye shall see first, the large and cheefe Foundation of your Feast, Fat Beefe.

                       Robert Herrick

Of all the delicates that Britons try
To please the palate and delight the eye,
Of all the sev'ral kinds of sumptuous fare,
There is none that can with apple pie compare.

                       William King

She give me some gingerbread made in cakes, like chocolate, very good, made by a friend.

                       Samuel Pepys

The knowledge of stilling is one pretty feat,
The waters be wholesome, the charges not great,
What timely thou gettest while summer doth last,
Think winter will help thee to spend it as fast.

                       Thomas Tusser

i

Foreword

A Small Brown Book

In a cardboard box, unearthed from Grandmother's attic, we found children's books, Moral Tales for the nursery, strange volumes of educational woodcuts . . . and amidst all this debris – a treasure; a collection of recipes assembled in 1655 for Henrietta Maria, widow of King Charles I.

THE QUEEN'S CLOSET OPENED

Incomparable secrets in physick, chyrurgery,
preserving and candying &c...

Printed for Nathaniel Brook
at the Angell in Cornhill, 1655

For years we valued this small brown book, 6 by 3 1/2 inches, falling apart with much use, the pages frayed at the corners and stained in places where it has come in too close contact with the cooking. We valued it chiefly for laughs, and at parties sometimes we would read the more peculiar recipes to our friends: "Master Rudstone's Posset" (even nicer with the 'long s' as Mafter Rudftone's Poffet), "To make Angelot, take a Gallon of Stroakings, and a pint of cream as it comes from the Cow ...", "Take a buttock of beefe ..."

Then, one day, someone gave us a basketful of quinces. What was to be done with this strange knobbly fruit? The recipe books didn't help – until it occurred to us to look into The Queen's Closet; and there was a recipe we've been using ever since, whenever there are quinces to be scrounged. Bit by bit other parts of the small brown book have been called into use, sometimes just as they stand (Sir Walter Raleigh's Strawberry Cordial does very well as it is), sometimes with judicious updating when "fine Roman Wormwood, Brook-lime, Smallage, Mother of Time" aren't so easy to come by.

Here are a few of those recipes in their original form, paired with modern equivalents, to provide some 80 rather unusual dishes which are easy for the accomplished cook and yet well within the reach of the less experienced. You may not wish to stew your ducks with oysters in a quart of claret, but you may be intrigued by the way they lived and ate in the seventeenth century; and the pictures have been chosen to show the ordinary and extraordinary things that were in use in the households of that time. The text and pictures recapture the feel and spirit of the seventeenth century and reconstruct the domestic lives of people living then. Life in the cottages and country houses was attuned to the seasons while in London the beautiful and barbaric simmered and bubbled together.

In the accompanying text much use has been made of the diaries of Samuel Pepys, John Evelyn and Celia Fiennes, and of the letters of the Paston and Smythe families. Amusing as it often is, this material is worth serious attention: we don't offer it for laughs any more, but as a reminder that even in the most turbulent of times we need to set a high value on the skills of the housekeeper and the cook.

Introduction

The Age of The Stuarts

Bliss was it in that dawn to be alive,
But to be young was very heaven!

Wordsworth, in those often-quoted lines, was looking back to the early days of the French Revolution, to a time when it seemed that a new age of freedom and equality was about to dawn. And there have been those who would want to apply his words not to France at the end of the eighteenth century, but to England at the beginning of the seventeenth. Not that there is very much to be said for the game of speculating when one would most have liked to live: but the reading of history, and the study of old documents (even of old cookery books) does set the imagination to work, and there are many reasons to think that of all periods of English history when it would be exciting, if not comfortable, to be alive, the age of the Stuarts would be hard to beat.

Queen Elizabeth died in 1603; and much that we think of as "Elizabethan" belongs in fact to the reign of James I who occupied the throne until 1625. So, if you were a Londoner born in 1600, you might – just – have seen the First Night of Macbeth. You could have heard John Donne preach, and known William Byrd at the height of his powers. You would have been Milton's contemporary, and Izaak Walton's, and have lived long enough, perhaps, to see Wren at work and to know Issac Newton, and to hear Purcell at Westminster Abbey. Boyle and Harvey belong to this age of discovery, as do the Pilgrim Fathers. It saw the founding of the Royal Society, and the building of the Royal Observatory, and the birth of two new nations in North America.

But alongside all this creative activity there was another aspect of seventeenth-century life which has to be kept in mind. It was a time of savagery and violence. In his book *Stuart England*, J. P. Kenyon says that contemporary foreigners regarded the English as an exceptionally excitable and blood-thirsty race and, according to one Dutch observer, "bold, courageous, ardent and cruel in war, but very inconstant, rash, vainglorious, light and deceiving". Admittedly, no-one living in the twentieth century has any right to talk glibly of the brutality of other ages; but there's no doubt that life in Stuart England faithfully reflected the violence which was erupting in Europe during the Thiry Years War, on the high seas where organized piracy was at its height, and throughout the Ottoman Empire. There was a particular virulence in the pamphleteering of those days, both religious and political. Extremism in language was matched by the savagery of public punishment and by the character of many public entertainments. Not that there was anything in this to mark the century as different from what preceded or followed it; but it needs to be remembered that the London of Van Dyck was a very foul city indeed, a rat-infested medieval place where plague was virtually an annual event. At least 150,000 people in England died of it between 1603 and 1665, when the total population cannot have been much more than 5 million.

Life for the poor was not so very different in any great city of the time – Paris, Vienna, Naples or Kiev. What was changing, and changing at great speed, was the worldwide distribution of trade and wealth and power. And with this change came the emergence, for the first time in Northern Europe, of a self-confident and creative middle-class. Three hundred years earlier the great trading centres of the Mediterranean had, as it were, broken out of the Middle Ages and given birth to the great movement which we call the Renaissance. That, too, had depended very largely on the patronage of commercial enterprise in centres like Florence and Venice: their wealth, and the wealth which they engendered for the ruling houses of the Italian city-states, depended for the most part either on trade with the east or on exploitation of the backwardness of the north in such matters as the wool trade. But with the opening up of trade with the west, and of the sea route to the Indies, the centre of power had by 1600 shifted north and west, to Lisbon and Bordeaux and Antwerp and London.

To see this shift at work, you only have to compare a painting by Rubens or Vermeer with any work of their southern contemporaries, and contrast the vigour of the one with the threadbare mannerisms of the other. Of course the influence of Italy remained immense; and it has to be said that it wasn't until the end of the eighteenth century that England produced a native tradition of painting which could stand beside that of the Low Countries. The same could be said of the other arts, except that in the field of architecture a succession of men of genius (Inigo Jones, Wren, Hawksmoor and the refugee Vanburgh) were able to take Italian models and transform them into a style particularly suited to a northern background.

It is an astonishing fact that during the years 1600–1700 England grew from isolation and near bankruptcy to be one of the most powerful nations in Europe and to rival the great autocratic regimes of France and Spain. It was a growth based on mercantile adventure, on what we would now describe as the exploitation of undeveloped countries through colonial expansion, yes, and through the slave trade. But whereas in France and Spain this expansion went to reinforce the power of an absolute monarchy, in Holland and in England it brought power where it had never been before: so that historians writing of this century can with equal truth call it The Age of Reason or The Age of Revolution – an age, at any rate, in which the Protestant bourgeois societies of the north were free to experiment with political ideas which didn't penetrate Catholic Europe until 150 years later. It was a freedom bought at the cost of a civil war in England and Wales, and of a violation of Ireland which has still not been healed; it required the beheading of a King and of an Archbishop, and social disruption on a large scale – all of which is beyond the scope of this book; except that, as always, it is in the minute details of private life, of how people ate and slept and brought up their children, that we can see some little way into the minds of those who have left records behind them, and perhaps guess something of what it was like for those whose lives go unrecorded.

Lawrence Stone, in his *The Causes of the English Revolution*, reminds us once again of the level of violence in the daily lives of the Elizabethans and Jacobeans. "The behaviour of the propertied classes, like that of the poor, was characterized by … ferocity, childishness and lack of self control" (quoted in J. P. Kenyon, *Stuart England*, pp. 44f). He makes a connection between delinquent behaviour and bad diet – a thought which lies very much within the scope of this book; and Professor Kenyon follows him in seeing Jacobean drama (the bloodcurdling productions of Webster and Ford, with their interest in rape, mutilation and incest) as reflecting a new climate of intrigue and insecurity. To be sure, the setting of this drama, as of the more light-hearted court masques, looks back to the palaces of the Italian Renaissance, but perhaps the scholars are right in suggesting that the lurid colours of the Jacobean stage reflect a deep malaise at the heart of Stuart England. It would be fascinating to explore the imagery of those poets, and to see if indigestible food really did lie at the root of the problem: whether the distempers that bred about the heart, the desperate imaginations and forced breath, the melancholy and the heat in the brain, are traceable in the end to the horrors of overeating and of too much sack. In which case the small brown book is not the least important historical document to have survived from the England of the Stuarts.

The Queen and Her Circle

Childhood and Marriage

Henrietta Maria was the youngest child of Henri IV of
France and his second wife, Maria de'Medici. She was
born at the Louvre in November 1609, her father
being at that time 56 years of age and her mother 36. It
was not a happy family to be born into. The king,
known to history as Henry of Navarre, was a man of
action, a swashbuckler of licentious habits, whose path
to the throne had involved him in changing his
religious allegiance three times and in unremitting
conflict with the nobles of France; in 1610 he was
assassinated by a fanatic said to be in the pay of the
Jesuits. The queen was a formidable woman, much
given to interference in the affairs of state: her regency
lasted only until 1617, at which point her son Louis XIII
at the age of 16 assumed the royal power and confined
her to her own house for 2 years. Her subsequent
intrigues brought her into conflict with Richelieu, and
in 1631 she was driven into exile in Brussels where she died in poverty 11 years later,
by which time her youngest daughter was in no position to help her.

Henrietta Maria

The little princess was from the first involved in the manoeuvres of dynastic
marriage. As early as 1620, when the French were anxious to draw England away
from a Spanish alliance, James I of England was approached with a proposal that she
should be married to Charles, Prince of Wales. The English ambassador in Paris, Sir
Edward Herbert, mentions that the child overheard a discussion to the effect that
her religion might raise difficulties, and quoted her as saying "A wife ought to have
no will but that of her husband". However, the proposal was dropped when
Charles, incognito, took a look at her on his way through Paris when he was going
to Madrid. Henrietta was only a rather small, skinny 13 year-old: Charles was 9 years
older, and he was on a glamorous cloak-and-dagger errand to court the Infanta of
Spain, with the Duke of Buckingham in support. In the event, the Spanish
negotiations came to nothing. The court of King Philip blew hot and cold, Charles
and Buckingham felt themselves humiliated, and the match was finally abandoned.

Discussions with the French court were re-opened under the agency of Viscount
Kensington who was sent to Paris and reported back that the princess was a "lovely,
sweet young creature". By May 1625 plans for the marriage were complete. Charles
was by now King, so he was married by proxy, and there was a delay of several
weeks before Henrietta Maria arrived in England and came face to face with her
husband.

Whatever else she inherited from her parents, she had all of her mother's force of
character and nothing of her father's religious ambivalence. She remained a
convinced and lifelong Catholic, and the orthodoxy of the French court led her to
see herself, from the start, as champion of the oppressed Catholics in England. It
was part of the marriage treaty that she should have her own chapel and chaplain in
each of the royal houses. She was attended, on her arrival in England, by a bishop
and 28 priests, and her large retinue of French servants immediately introduced a
sizeable Catholic element into the royal entourage.

Marie de Medici, either because she was sick or because she was reluctant to let her daughter go, put a brake on the travel arrangements. They delayed for a fortnight at Amiens, after which Henrietta and her attendants made their own way to Boulogne (where she saw the sea for the first time and hated it ever after) and then to Dover.

It seems not to have occurred to anyone that the new Queen should learn even the rudiments of the English language. Admittedly the King, like any educated man, could speak French well; but there's no doubt that the Queen's early years in England were lonely and unhappy, partly because Charles was a shy and reserved man, much influenced by the Duke of Buckingham, but equally because she herself remained cocooned within her French household, isolated by differences of language and religion for which her upbringing had done nothing to prepare her. It reflects no small credit on both Charles and Henrietta that these early drawbacks were eventually overcome and gave way to a devotion and loyalty that survived right up to the King's death, and beyond.

The Court: Favourites, Entertainments, Palaces

It was something of a family joke among the Queen's children that she always had bad luck at sea. The crossing from Boulogne to Dover was appalling, and took 24 hours. The King was not there to meet her. He was staying more comfortably at Canterbury. So she and her large party of followers were quartered for the night in Dover Castle, a cold and inhospitable lodging. When Charles arrived the next morning she was at breakfast, but she rose to meet her husband and began the formal speech which royal etiquette demanded: "Sire, I am come unto your Majesty's country to be made use of and commanded by you ..." but couldn't continue because of her tears. Charles is reported to have been very gentle with her, and said "that he would be no longer master himself than whilst he was a servant to her". There was some embarrassment about the meal that followed, after the French party had been duly presented: pheasant and venison were served, the King carved it, but as the Eve of St John's Day was a prescribed fast for the Catholics, the Queen's Confessor stood disapprovingly behind the Queen's chair throughout the meal. The feast which followed next day at Canterbury, after the ratification of the marriage, was not much more of a success, as the French were unaware of Charles' financial difficulties and regarded the provision as very far from the splendour they had expected.

1625 was a bad year for the plague. It is estimated that 41,000 people died of it. So it was thought wise that the Queen should come to London by water. The Fleet was at anchor in the Thames, so an inspection was arranged, and guns were fired in salute from the men of war and from the Tower garrison as the royal barge made its way up the river. They landed at Denmark House, where Somerset House now stands: the earlier building had belonged to Charles' mother, Anne of Denmark, and many improvements had been made by Inigo Jones, the court architect and stage-designer who was to work so closely with the new Queen in the years which followed. However, the bridal pair stayed only a short time in London – long enough for the French to confirm their view that Charles' hospitality was the more meagre as it was compared with that of the Duke of Buckingham, whose private wealth was enormous, and whose banquet in their honour was magnificent in the extreme.

Nothing more was done, for the moment, to introduce the Queen to her subjects. Her life was to remain enclosed within the circles of the Court, and more particularly within the French coterie which formed her part of it. Charles did make one requirement, that she should take on the English form of her name and be known as

Queen Mary. This was in itself unfortunate, as it evoked memories of Bloody Mary and the persecutions associated with the reign of the last Catholic monarch. In due course a compromise was reached, and history has always known her by the latinized form of her name, as Henrietta Maria.

The Court of King James I had been in some respects deplorable. The King had a penchant for good-looking young men, and had lavished his attentions and a great deal of money first on James Hay and Robert Ker, ennobling them as viscount and earl respectively. His relationship with both was overtly sexual, and of no great political significance. George Villiers was another matter altogether. From his first appearance at Court in 1614 his sights were set on political power; within 9 years he had acquired a dukedom, the first to go outside the Royal Family since 1485, huge wealth, and ascendancy not only over the ageing King but over the heir to the throne, whose tastes certainly did not lie in the same direction as his father's. Charles indeed was something of a prig. He was sober and chaste and loyal, and certainly not the kind of man to be swept off his feet by Buckingham's charm or swayed by Buckingham's ambition. It's all the more remarkable that he deferred so much to his father's favourite: regrettable, too, in that that deference above all else hindered the growth of love and respect between the new King and his young wife. Not until Buckingham's death by assassination in 1628 did Charles seek from the Queen that affection which they both needed.

Meanwhile Charles was engaged in bringing a new respectability to the Court. It has been often pointed out that hints of this reform are to be found in the literature of the time, as in John Webster's *The Duchess of Malfi* (1623).

> *In seeking to reduce both State and People*
> *To a fix'd order, their judiciouse King*
> *Begins at home.*

The style of the Court, however, did little to reduce Charles' debts, which he inherited to the tune of some £900,000. His household comprised around 300 courtiers, with about twice that number of servants to provide the basic services of food, drink, light, heat, cleaning and laundry. There were over 200 Beefeaters in the royal bodyguard, and nearer 300 in the royal stables, made all the more necessary by the constant travelling which was so much a part of Court life. It is estimated that during the 1630s the upkeep of the household averaged more than a quarter of a million pounds a year, nearly half of the King's income. The assumption is that a large amount of this money was misappropriated by the King's servants and courtiers.

In spite of Charles' personal austerity life at Court was lived in the grand manner. As at the French Court, meals were served to the Royal Family in public by pages on bended knee. A picture by Gerard Houckeest shows Charles and Henrietta Maria dining in a vast marble-floored hall, with courtiers and King Charles spaniels standing around. The King and Queen sit at the centre of the table. In a letter from London, the painter Rubens writes "All the leading nobles here live on a most sumptuous scale and spend money lavishly. Splendour and liberality are the first considerations at Court. In this place I find none of the crudeness that one might expect from a place so remote from Italian elegance".

Remote, too, from the influence of the French Court; so that when after a year of marriage Charles told his wife that all her French household including the bishop and the priests must leave, the Queen was deeply hurt and angry, accusing her husband of breaking the marriage contract. Charles was adamant, not least because Buckingham had contrived to make mischief among the Queen's retainers and had fostered dangerous enmities. The bishop had to go, and 29 priests and 410 male and female attendants. They took with them £11,000 in wages, jewels of almost twice that value, and (so it was said) all the Queen's prodigious trousseau. Even if that does sound rather like cutting off one's nose to spite one's face, it was no doubt a wise move on Charles' part; but not until Buckingham's death was the rift with the Queen made good.

In spite of these setbacks the Queen didn't lack for amusements. As patrons of the arts the Stuart kings carried on the grandest traditions of the Renaissance princes, being well aware of the political as well as the cultural value of the creative artist. Peter Paul Rubens gave distinction to the English Court: he was also a shrewd propagandist, and when he came to England in 1630 he painted a grandiloquent picture, *St George and the Dragon*, in which the King is portrayed as the patron Saint of England, having just slain the dragon of war, and in the act of rescuing the fair maiden who bears a strong resemblance to Henrietta Maria, so bringing peace to his realm. It's never easy in Baroque art to distinguish the political from the merely decorative. Certainly Rubens' great decorative scheme in the Banqueting Hall at Whitehall has strong political ingredients (he was, after all, accredited ambassador to the English Court) and glorifies the House of Stuart almost to the point of absurdity: but as well as being a statement about monarchy, Inigo Jones' great hall was a place of delight, the scene of those pageants and masques in which dancing and music were allied to Jones' talents as a stage designer to provide Court entertainment of a high quality. The Queen took great delight in all this activity, and there are many accounts, both favourable and disapproving, of the part she played in them. It's worth remembering that at the very time when Monteverdi in Venice was creating the very first European operas, Henry Lawes at the English Court was founding a tradition of musical drama which was to come into full flower with Locke and Purcell in the next generation.

Take 1632, for example. The influence of Buckingham had in the past 4 years been succeeded by a strong and growing bond between the King and Queen. The Banqueting Hall was newly decorated, and there was to be the usual succession of diversions after Christmas. On 8 January, the King's Masque, *Albion's Triumph*, was presented with a formality which suited Charles' character: the setting was ideal for such a purpose, Roman settings were devised on a heroic scale, and the King was presented as conquering through the power of love and bringing peace and prosperity to his country.

More in keeping with the Queen's character was the Queen's Masque, which followed on Shrove Tuesday. For weeks before, Henrietta Maria and Inigo Jones worked together devising costumes and stage designs. Jones himself was evidently something of a martinet, and insisted on leaving as little as possible of the work to his assistants, so that the whole effect was clearly the work of one man. There is a famous account of him by his contemporary Ben Johnson;

> *He will join with no man,*
> *Though he be a joiner – in design he calls it,*
> *He must be sole inventor.*

When the night of the performance arrived the curtain went up to reveal a rural scene with fountains spouting water into basins, slender trees and flowers. Fourteen children whose parents were members of the Court danced a saraband before joining their parents in the audience. Then came the pageantry of Jones' famous cloud machines. First out of the heavens came eight spheres seated on a cloud, all musicians with Nicholas Lanier the composer at their head. Two more clouds brought 8 stars down to earth, followed by 5 more. Finally, the Queen herself, arrayed as Divine Beauty in a golden chariot studded with jewels, and wearing a dress of blue embossed with stars, her head haloed with light, appeared. As she stepped out of her chariot, the clouds were taken back into the heavens and the celestial apparitions joined the Queen in a great tableau of blue and silver, with at least 50 people on stage. It was agreed that all including the Queen had excelled themselves and demonstrated the magnificence of the English Court. The cost of such a spectacle was, of course, enormous and often repeated: excellent for the international prestige of the English monarchy, but certainly a contributory factor in the growing alienation of the monarchy from its subjects.

Indeed, there were many who disapproved of the Queen's involvement in such activities. She was widely regarded as light-hearted and frivolous, and was blamed for attracting the less dependable elements among the members of the Court. Certainly the courtiers themselves vied with one another in writing plays, masques and verses in the Queen's honour. In 1632 Walter Montague, probably the W. M. who compiled the small brown book, wrote *The Shepherd's Pastoral* for the Queen to act on the King's birthday, and it was her part in this which evoked from the Puritan William Prynne his well-known attack upon women on the stage, *Histrio-Mastix – The Players' Scourge*, in which he railed against female actors and called them whores in a book of a thousand pages. Because this was seen as a reflection on the virtue of the Queen, he was sentenced to have his book burned by the common hangman, his ears were cropped, he was fined £5,000, expelled from Oxford University and from Lincoln's Inn, and imprisoned "in perpetuity" in the Tower of London. (He was in trouble again later for his attacks on William Laud, but emerged from the Tower in 1640 and ended his life as an ardent royalist: Charles II, who had a sense of humour rather stronger than his father's, made him Keeper of the Tower Records ...) Prynne's fellow lawyers at Lincoln's Inn were clearly embarrassed by all this; they presented themselves before the Queen, with a masque in protest against the Puritan view of the theatre, and Henrietta Maria not only received them gracefully but actually danced with some of the performers.

Whitehall was usually the scene for the diversions of the Court as well as for more formal state occasions. By a savage irony it was to be the setting for the execution of the King. For the most part Whitehall palace retained much the same appearance as it had in Tudor times. The grounds stretched from the Thames to St James' Park, though a public road ran through it from Charing Cross to Westminster. An irregular collection of buildings, mostly of weathered red brick, gave access to the river where there was a rambling mass of State Apartments with privy stairs to the Thames, a Great Hall and a Chapel, surrounded by open space which was laid out in gardens and included a cockpit and a tilting-yard. Not far away to the west is the old palace of St James, built by Henry VIII as a hunting-lodge. To the north, a little way downstream from Whitehall, was Denmark House which Charles gave to his Queen shortly after they were married. This was the cluster of buildings in which the Court was housed while the King was in London. Different rulers had different patterns of life: Queen Elizabeth was for ever on the move, up and down her kingdom, whereas James I restricted his movements to visits to Royston and Newmarket.

It seems that until the outbreak of the Civil War Charles and his family spent the greater part of the year in and around London. There was a cluster of country palaces to which the Court could withdraw when the weather was warm and when pestilence was rife. Hampton Court lies a few miles up river. Nonsuch was at Ewell in Surrey, and Oatlands at Weybridge. There was Theobalds at Cheshunt in nearby Hertfordshire, Sheen at Richmond-on-Thames, and Windsor Castle not very far

Windsor Castle (Bodleian, Douce Prints a 24., plate 7)

distant. The old palace at Greenwich dated from the fifteenth century, but was rebuilt for Henrietta Maria to the magnificent designs of Inigo Jones and was completed by 1633. The state rooms are situated on the *piano nobile*, the first floor, and are reached by an extremely grand circular staircase. (The building now houses the National Maritime Museum.)

It is remarkable that, apart from Greenwich in its new guise, none of these great houses has survived except Cardinal Wolsey's palace at Hampton Court, and Henry VIII's lodge at St James' – still officially the Court of the Monarch. Nonsuch was given by Charles II to Lady Castlemaine, who dismantled it, and only an avenue of lime trees remains to show where that great house was. Oatlands was destroyed during the Civil War. Theobalds was demolished by Cromwell in 1651, and Sheen, the favourite dwelling of Edward III, Henry V and Henry VIII, was sold in 1649 and allowed to fall into disrepair; only a gateway and part of a courtyard have survived.

The Royal Family

Vistors to the great Van Dyck exhibition at the National Portrait Gallery, some years ago, inevitably came away with a strong impression of Charles I as a family man. History books and biographies never fail to mention this quality as the one clear characteristic in an otherwise baffling personality. And yet the early years of the royal marriage could hardly have been less propitious. At first there was a real power-struggle at Court between the French faction surrounding the Queen and the Buckingham connection apparently dominating the King. After the disappearance of both parties, the King and Queen could easily have retreated into positions of mutual hostility and isolation, and it is a remarkable fact that this did not happen, despite their very different temperaments and their incompatible religious beliefs.

It may well be that one of the main advantages to the King and Queen derived from the absence of interference from the Queen's own family. Relationships with her brother Louis XIII were never cordial, and the French King was at loggerheads with the Queen Mother. Marie de Medici was an unattractive woman, by all accounts, and her prolonged visit to the English Court in 1638–41 was not a success. Indeed, during that time popular feeling against the Queen's party ran high, but that did not deter Charles and Henrietta Maria from their intention to build a life together and to raise what was, considering the troubled times and the fashions of the age, a remarkably happy and united family.

It was while walking in one of the galleries at Greenwich Palace that the Queen found herself suddenly in the middle of a dog-fight. One of the dogs jumped up and tore her dress. She ran to her apartments, and it was soon evident that her first child would be born ten weeks prematurely. All arrangements had been made for her to go to St James' for her lying-in, and there was no physician in attendance. Courtiers rushed to the nearest village for help, but when the local midwife heard that she was to attend upon the Queen she fainted with fright. So the child was born without any skilled attention and when the physician did arrive both mother and son were in grave danger. The King quickly had the baby baptized by his own Chaplain, Dr Webb, and named Charles James; but he died 2 hours later, and that same night his tiny coffin was covered with a black pall, carried to Westminster Abbey by 6 sons of earls accompanied by 6 sons of barons, and laid to rest beside his grandfather James I.

A year later this disappointment was happily followed by the birth of an heir to the throne. The future Charles II was born on 29 May 1630. There followed 7 more children, and as was always the case in those days some survived and some did not. James Duke of York, who was to succeed his brother as James II was born in 1633. Two years earlier the Royal Family's eldest daughter had been born, the Princess Mary who at the age of 10 was married to William Prince of Orange and in due course became the mother of the future King William III. Subsequently 3 daughters followed, none of whom lived to more than 4 years of age, for smallpox was a terrible destroyer of young life and it also claimed a third son, Henry Duke of Gloucester who died of it in 1660. Finally in 1644 the Queen gave birth to their youngest child, Henrietta Anne, deeply beloved by all the family as "Minette": her upbringing was in France, during the exile, and she grew up a Roman Catholic and was married to Phillippe, Duc d'Orleans, the younger brother of Louis XIV. Hers was not a happy marriage, and she died in 1670 shortly after her mother.

No family in those days, rich or poor, was without its share of tragedies. After the King's death, when she was in exile at the French Court, Henrietta Maria was known as *La Reine Malheureuse*, and it may be that from such a point of view her earlier life took on in retrospect a glow which it didn't have at the time. But she certainly said of the 1630s that at that time she was "the happiest and most fortunate of queens", and there appears to be no reason to contradict her. Only English was spoken in the presence of the Royal Children, and it did seem at last as though the French princess who on her arrival in England had been dubbed "The Popish Brat" had found fulfilment as a wife and as mother of a line of English kings.

The Civil War

It is well beyond the scope of this book to trace the progress of the Civil War from its origins in the King's struggle with Parliament, through the disasters in Ireland, to the final scene on the scaffold. Even the Queen's part in the conflict is much disputed. She certainly seems to have been engaged quite literally in back-stairs intrigue at any rate from 1638 onwards, and it has been said by those unsympathetic to her that her support for Charles, heartening though it may have been at the domestic level, served to aggravate the political blunders of his reign.

The bare facts are that in the first 4 years of Charles' reign three parliaments were summoned and dissolved, amid increasing opposition from landed gentry like Pym and Hampden, as well as from Puritan nobles like Warwick and Essex. From 1629 to 1640 Charles reigned without calling a parliament, counting on support from the much hated courts of the Star Chamber and the High Commission.

Money was always a problem and the King was always seeking more from the Treasury. He extended the Ship Tax to include all cities, not just ports and this was met by Hampden's passive resistance and Pym's more vocal one.

Archbishop Laud

Archbishop Laud, with Charles's backing, attempted to anglicize the Scottish Church and met with riots and then open rebellion. Charles was forced to call parliament, and two met in 1640; the Short Parliament which met for 3 weeks, and the Long Parliament which outlived Charles. It met and passed a bill by which an existing parliament might not be dissolved except by its own consent, and also to pronounce Strafford's doom.

It 1632 Strafford had been made Lord Deputy of Ireland and had thoroughly reorganized the army, reduced piracy and lawlessness, and introduced and nurtured a flax industry. Seven years later he was made Earl of Strafford and Lord Lieutenant of Ireland and one of the King's principal advisers. The rebellion in Scotland began to spread over the border into the north of England, and Strafford offered to lead an Irish army against Scotland. The offer was pounced on by Pym and his followers and Strafford was impeached and lodged in the Tower; he was charged with "cumulative treason" for "he had an army in Ireland which he could employ to reduce this Kingdom". The King did not save him and he was executed on Tower Hill in 1641. Laud followed him to the scaffold in 1645.

Meanwhile a party was forming in the House of Commons of men who revolted from the sweeping changes that menaced both Church and State, and Pym's Grand Remonstrance justified their fears. Charles seemed to justify the Grand Remonstrance by his attempt to arrest 5 members of the House, but they had been warned and had fled just in time to escape. His attempt to arrest them was dictated by the knowledge of an impending impeachment of the Queen. She managed to escape to

Holland in March 1641 and there sold many of her jewels and raised money for the royalist cause. By the end of August 1642 England was in the grip of Civil War. The Queen in exile in Holland was almost pennyless and ends a letter to the King: "Adieu, my dear heart, I am going to take my supper, and as it has cost money I must not let it get spoiled."

She managed to assemble several shiploads of arms, some professional soldiers and money, and set sail for England on 10 January of the next year. The wind began to rise and by midnight had turned into a tempest. The ships were driven to and fro near the Dogger Sands and for 9 days and nights the Queen's ladies were strapped into their bunks, unable to sleep and fearing death by drowning at any minute. When they were not being sea-sick they made their last confessions which, we are told, the Queen found most interesting. She comforted them and by showing remarkable courage prevented panic. At last they had to turn back and land again in Holland.

When they sailed again 10 days later they could not land at Newcastle as they intended but had to put in at Bridlington. Lodgings were found for the Queen in a thatched cottage on the quay. She was woken at 4 o'clock in the morning by a bombardment from Parliamentary ships which had seen her ships enter the bay. The Queen and her ladies ran inland and sheltered in a ditch "like those at Newmarket" she afterwards wrote to the King. As the ladies sat there canon-balls whistled overhead sometimes showering them with earth until the tide went out and the ships had to withdraw out of range. She wrote to the King giving him an exact description of the bombardment while it was all fresh in her mind ending by saying she hoped now to have something to eat "having taken nothing today but three eggs and slept very little".

The Queen rode to meet her husband and often ate with her soldiers. Many fine estates had been sequestered to provide funds for one side or the other with towns, villages and even families divided in their loyalties.

Almost all the way along her route the records remain silent about her stay in case the Parlimentary troops came later with reprisals. The otherwise well-kept Minute Book of the Stratford upon Avon Corporation has entries that are short and spasmodic during this troubled time and no mention was made of the royal visitor who spent a night at New Place with Susanna Hall, Shakespeare's daughter. It is only deep in the Chamberlain's account book that there are entries showing that payment was made for bread, geese, beans, beer, three hens, eight chickens and four quail, and a present of cakes costing £5 for the Queen.

The King and Queen met after 18 months separation, and rode into Oxford where the Court and some of the Royalist troops were quartered. Oxford had declared itself Royalist and given accommodation and much support in the form of College plate which was coined into money to enable the King to maintain his forces. Evelyn wrote in his diary that he was glad that he had given his College books for the Library instead of plate: "The Plate was gon but my books remaine". He also mentions a relative, Sir John Glanvill, formally Speaker of the House of Commons, who now lived in his Gate-house at Broad Hinton "his very faire dwelling house, having been burnt by his owne hands, to prevent the Rebels making a Garrison of it".

Parliamentary armies were in the home counties under the command of Essex. Men like Colonel Fiennes of Newton Toney, John Hampden of Great Hampden, Thomas Smyth of Ashton Court, and the three Popham brothers had raised troops in their neighbourhoods and paid for their training and arms. As the Civil War went on they became better trained and disciplined. The Royalist troops rode out of Oxford under Prince Rupert, the King's nephew, for quick skirmishes which sometimes developed into battles. It was at one of these at Chalgrove Field that John Hampden was fatally wounded, and the loss of his quiet leadership was grievous to the Parliamentarians.

The Queen found that she was expecting her ninth child and was not at all well; by the Spring her health was causing alarm and it was decided that she should try the curative waters at Bath.

Charles accompanied her as far as Abingdon and there they said their last farewell. She was terrified of being taken by the enemy and only stayed in Bath a few days before moving on to Exeter. Here, on 16 June 1644, desperately ill, she gave birth to Henrietta Anne. Parliamentary troops were drawing nearer and only 15 days after her confinement the Queen had to leave with only Sir John Winter, one lady and her confessor on a hazardous 6 day journey to Pendennis Castle at Falmouth. The castle was garrisoned by Colonel Sir John Arundell of Trerice who wrote, "the most worne and weak pitiful creature in the world, the poor Queene, shifting for one hour's life longer".

Before embarking for France, she wrote to Charles ending the letter: "I am giving you the strongest proof of love that I can give. I am hazarding my life, that I may not incommode your affairs. Adieu, my dear heart".

After an appalling crossing being chased and shot at by the enemy and losing a good deal of the ship's rigging the Queen landed in France.

The Kings Death

The Villanie of the Rebels proceeding now so far as to Trie, Condemne, and Murder our excellent King, the thirtieth of this Moneth, struck me with such horror that I kept the day of his Martyrdom a fast, and would not be present at that excecrable wickedness.

So wrote one man and probably expressed the feelings of shock and repulsion of many others. For England the struggle for democracy came about 150 years earlier than for other countries in Europe, and the beheading of a King had tremendous repercussions.

Charles I walked from St James' to the Banqueting House with the Bishop of London, Bishop Juxon, and there received the Sacrament from him. A platform had been erected outside so that the King could walk through one of the windows directly on to it for his execution. It was ironic and heart-rending that this should be the scene of his execution when he had spent so much thought, time and expense on the adorning of the Banqueting House, and it had been the setting of so many magnificent and happy times for him and his Queen.

A crowd had been waiting all the morning of that cold January day in 1649; a silent crowd, unlike the crowds of the French revolution a little more than a hundred years later. He took off his black cloak and doublet, and gave his gloves and his badge of the Garter which he had been wearing to the Bishop before kneeling to meet his death, with his cryptic last word: "Remember".

So England passed from the "divine right of Kings" type of Monachy into the period of the Commonwealth and democracy. When Charles II was restored to the throne of England 11 years later it was Parliament that had the power and not the Monarchy.

Henrietta Maria was devastated by the news and retired into the convent in the Faubourg St Jacques. The regular routine of the convent life helped her through the first tragic months of shock and bereavement.

When she emerged from the convent she was wearing the mourning that she kept for the next 20 years until her death. Her black dresses paid little heed to fashion, but were always the same with a full skirt sweeping the ground, a fitting bodice and

Banqueting House, Whitehall

lace at the throat and wrists. She wore little jewellery, just her beautiful pearls or her diamond cross. She wore either a cap with a widow's peak and a veil, or a cap with black lace round the brow; her hair was arranged in ringlets at the side of her face. Only once, in 1660, did she go back to England to visit her son and to see old friends and then she retired to her native France.

Who Was W.M.?

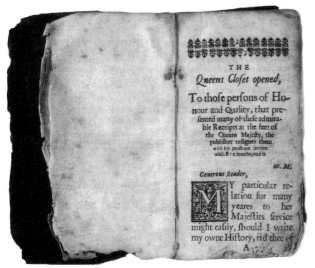

Incomparable Secrets ... as they were presented to the Queen by the most Experienced persons of our Times, many whereof were honoured with her own practice, when she was pleased to descend to these more private Recreations ... Never before published ... Transcribed from the true Copies of her Majesties own Receipt-Book by W. M. one of her late servants. Vivit post funera virtus.

So reads the title-page of the Small Brown Book. There are various questions which arise from it. The latin motto says that goodness survives death: but whose death? The Queen was still alive in 1655 when the book was published, and so presumably was the compiler. Is the volume, therefore, offered as a kind of tribute to the late King? "Never before published ..." yet in the Address to the Reader the publication is itself excused by the fact that pirated copies of the Queen's papers were already in circulation. Above all, who was W.M.?

There's no means of knowing. But he does speak of his own "particular relation over many yeares to her Majesties service", and of "the original papers being most of them preserved in my own hands, being kept as so many Reliques". This suggests a more than usually close association with the Royal Household. And there is nobody who fits more closely into this profile than one who by the age of 20 was already employed in confidential business for the Royal Family, and in later life was Confessor and Almoner to the Queen both in England and in exile -- Walter Montagu.

The Dictionary of National Biography, in its article on Montagu, paints a fascinating picture of the career of a Stuart courtier. Born in or about 1603, Walter was the second son of Sir Henry Montagu, first Earl of Manchester. Baptized in the parish of St Botolph Aldgate, in the City of London, he was admitted at the age of 13 as a Fellow Commoner of Sidney Sussex College, Cambridge (Oliver Cromwell's college – though the future Lord Protector was 4 years his senior) but shortly afterwards went abroad in order to study foreign languages and "other qualifications proper for a nobleman".

On his return to England Montagu was received at Court and was very soon employed by Buckingham in the first, secret negotiations with the French King in the matter of the proposed royal marriage. Nothing came of this first round of talks, but he was given the very generous sum of £200 as a reward for "special service". A year later, in 1625, when he was still a very young man, he was again in France conducting delicate negotiations over the return of some English ships which had been impounded by the French, and returned with guarantees of restitution and with promises of peace. He was evidently required (by Buckingam?) to play something of a double game, as in 1627 he was in Lorraine and Italy with the express purpose of making mischief against the French. His report to Charles I made clear that in the event of war he could look for no help in that direction; and on his way home he was arrested on the orders of Cardinal Richelieu and spent some time in the Bastille before he was released. Even so, his work was clearly of value to the King, as on his return he was granted £1,100, and an extra expense allowance of £400, "for His Majesty's Secret Service in France". Apparently he remained *persona grata* at the French Court, as he was resident in Paris after 1633, living at the British Ambassador's house.

It was at this point, after a visit to Loudun to witness the exorcism of a group of Ursuline nuns, that Montagu became a Roman Catholic. He returned to England to justify this decision to his family, and then left for Rome where he joined the Oratorians and made his submission to Pope Urban VIII in person. His letter to his father explaining his actions was widely circulated in the Queen's circle at London, and when he was ordained priest he was allowed to return to England where he was often to be seen at Denmark House, and seems to have been allied with attempts to involve the Queen in political activity. As the political scene in England grew more tense, Montagu found himself increasingly employed by the Queen's party in a variety of intrigues. He went with Kenelm Digby on a fund-raising tour of Catholic sympathizers to collect money for Charles' army, and in 1641 was ordered by Parliament to give an account of this collection, being required as a result to retire into France.

By 1643 he was again working in the King's cause, slipping into England "in a disguised habit, his face all besmutched, and having on a very great perriwig". At Rochester he was arrested and kept in close arrest in the Tower of London for being in posssession of letters sealed with the arms of France and addressed to the King and Queen of England. He seems to have spent his imprisonment in theological disputations, subsequently published; and in due course was allowed to travel, "on good bail", to Tunbridge Wells to drink the waters. It is remarkable that even after the King's death Montagu, a known Catholic and agent of the Crown, was still at liberty: not until the end of August 1649 was he, together with Kenelm Digby and Sir John Winter the Queen's Secretary, exiled on pain of death.

In exile he prospered. The Queen Dowager of France made him Abbot of St Martin de Pontoise, and for a time he enjoyed the patronage of the all-powerful Cardinal Mazarin and of other influential figures at Court. But his main work was as confidant and adviser to the English Royal Family in exile. Henry, Duke of Gloucester was in particular committed to his charge, though he never succeeded in winning over the young duke to the Catholic cause. In 1660, at considerable risk, he paid a secret visit to his brother Edward, by then Earl of Manchester, but otherwise he played little part in the events of his native country after the Restoration. When the English exiles left the French Court Montagu's own influence declined: he was required to resign his abbacy in 1670, though he remained in receipt of its revenues until his death in the Hôpital des Incurables in 1677.

Montagu was the author of a small body of published verse, now quite forgotten. He was also, in his earlier days, much in demand as a writer of plays and masques for the entertainment of his patrons. We read of "The Accomplish'd Woman: translated from the French and dedicated to the Duchess of Buckingham", and "The Shepherd's Paradise", a comedy privately acted before the late King Charles by the Queen's Majesty.

Whether or not it was this Walter Montagu who as "W.M." caused the Queen's papers to be printed, his career gives us a fascinating glimpse of the life of one of her most trusted servants – a picture made up of courage, intrigue and great personal loyalty to the Stuart cause.

To dress Oysters

Take Oysters and open them and save the Liquor, and when you have opened so many as you please, add to this Liquor some white wine, wherein you must wash your Oysters one by one very clean and lay them in another Dish; then strain to them that mixed wine and Liquor wherein they were washed, adding a little more wine to them with an Onyon divided with some salt and pepper, so done, cover the dish and stew them till they be more then half done, then take them and the Liquor, and poure it into a frying panne, wherein they must fry a pretty while, then put into them a good peice of sweet butter, and fry them therein so much longer, in the mean time you must have beaten the yelks of some Eggs, as four or five to a quart of Oysters: These Eggs must be beaten with some Vinegar, wherein you must put some minced parsley and Nutmeg finely scraped, and put therein the Oysters in the panne, which must still be kept stirring least the Liquor make the Eggs cruddle, let this all have a good wame on the fire, and serve it up.

Izaak Walton, certainly the most famous English fisherman, lived in the seventeenth century, and lived to be 90. He wrote *The Compleat Angler, or the Contemplative Man's Recreation,* the first edition of which appeared in 1653, and had 13 chapters. It was most popular and so it grew, and by the fifth edition in 1676 it had 21 chapters. It is a discourse on fish and fishing and English rivers, fish-ponds, rods, lines and flies. It is interspersed with idyllic glimpses of country life, quotations of quaint old verses, songs and moral reflections and has enormous charm. It is still read, used and enjoyed by fishermen as the country lore holds good, and fishing has the biggest number of participants of any recreation in England today.

Izaak Waltons's house, Winchester

Baked Cod and Smoked Mussels

1¹/₂ lb/675 g Cod fillet or 4 frozen portions (thawed)
1 tin of smoked mussels
¹/₂ pint/275 ml milk
salt and pepper
¹/₂ teaspoon sweet basil
1 tablespoon plain flour

Prepare fish and put it in an ovenproof dish with the milk; sprinkle over the salt, pepper and basil. Bake in the oven at 325°F (170°C) Gas Mark 3 for about 15 minutes or until cooked through depending on thickness.

In the meantime drain the oil from the tin of mussels into a pan and add flour and blend into the oil; if there is not enough oil then add a little butter. Cook and stir well over the heat for 2 minutes.

When the fish is cooked put it onto a serving dish and keep hot. Add the milk from the pan gradually to the flour mixture, beat well and cook until it thickens into a creamy sauce. Cut the mussels in half and add them to the sauce and just bring back to the boil. Pour over the fish, garnish with parsley and serve.Baked Cod and Smoked Mussels

But fishing was not always angling. John Evelyn describes how he was journeying to Stonehenge and stopped on the way to dine at one of his uncle's farms in a valley "most sweetly water'd, abounding in Trowts". He writes of how they catch the trout "by Speare in the night" while they come up to a light set in the stern of the boat.

Fish made very acceptable gifts and we know that a sturgeon was given to the Mayor of Cambridge by his two Treasurers for Christmas in 1664; it cost them 1 shilling. On a visit of the Judge the Mayor and Aldermen sent him a present of food which included 6 perch, a pike and 2 eels.

Eels formed a very large part of people's diet in the low-lying areas where they were found. They were trapped in long wicker baskets made out of willow twigs, baited with worms soaked in verbena oil, and were either cooked at once or smoked. They were sold in 'sticks' of 25 or would be used for barter or for paying rents. Eels played an important part in the economy of the Fens where they were to be found in vast quantities. The monks of Ely paid 4,000 eels a year for the right to quarry stone at Barnack, near Peterborough, to use to build their monastery at Ely, and it was said that "Ely Cathedral was built of Eels".

Eel skins taken in the springtime were dried, greased and then polished to keep them supple and made into garters. They were used by both men and women and tied above the knee. They were said to prevent rheumatism and were a most necessary precaution in the wet low-lying Fens.

To dresse Flounders

Flea off the black skin, and scowr the fish over on that side with a knife, lay them in a dish, and poure on them some Vinegar, and strew good store of salt, let them lye for half an hour, in the mean time set on the fire some water with a little white Wine, Garlick and sweet Herbs as you please, putting into it the Vinegar and salt wherein they lay, when it boyles put in the biggest fish, then the next till all be in, when they are boyled, take them out and drain them very well, then draw some sweet butter thick, and mix with it some Anchoves shred small, which being dissolved in the butter, pour it on the fish, strewing a little sliced Nutmeg, and minced Oranges and Barbaries.

We know from household accounts that breakfasts were simple but nourishing; ale, bread and fish seem to figure largely. Barrels of oysters were bought and in the autumn large stocks of salt fish were kept by a sizeable household for the whole winter's use. Cheese was also a standby for breakfasts. Working men usually did 2 or 3 hours work before the first meal of the day and we read of Pepys meeting his friends in alehouses for this meal at about 9 o'clock. Sometimes in summer he was up at 5 or 6 o'clock but then he was very industrious. He often chose bread, ale and oysters, and cheese is mentioned if it was especially good. What his wife ate at home we are not told.

New Inn, Gloucester

Baked Anchovy Pie

12 oz/350 g white fish
1 tin, 1³/₄ oz/50 g anchovies
2 large onions
6 potatoes
White pepper
¹/₂ teaspoon thyme
2 oz/50 g butter
7 oz/200 ml thin cream or top of the milk

Melt the butter and any oil from the tin of anchovies in a pan and gently cook the onions thinly sliced. Peel the potatoes and then slice them thinly.

Grease a pie dish and put in a layer of potatoes, then a layer of onions, white fish in little pieces and anchovies; sprinkle with pepper and thyme. Repeat, and finally put a layer of potatoes on the top. Pour over the cream and dot with a little butter.

Bake in the oven at 400°F (200°C) Gas Mark 6 for about an hour until the potatoes are cooked, but watch that the top does not get too brown; if this seems likely then cover with kitchen foil.

A note from a Slave Trader's log book at Sligo in 1600 says; "As to the smoak we saw, it might have been travellers who were rosting of oysters and shell fish on the shore". Shellfish was often eaten as soon as it was caught by making a fire on the shore and heating some flat stones and placing the oysters or mussels on the stones and so roasting them by the fire. They would open in the heat. On the East coast of America clams are collected and baked on the shore and at places in Maine it is possible to see a layer of clam shells near the top of a cliff left over from an Indian settlement.

Izaak Walton gives a "minnow Tansie" recipe which could make good use of a small boy's fishing. "And in the Spring they make them excellent Minnow tansies – for being washed well in salt, and their heads and tails cut off and their guts taken out, they prove excellent for that use, that is being fried with yolks of eggs, the flowers of cowslips and of primroses and a little tansy; thus used they make a dainty dish of Meat".

George Borrow in the nineteenth century described in his book *Wild Wales* a breakfast he had while on a walking tour. He was surprised and delighted to find it included a pot of hare, pot of trout and a pot of shrimps. Potted meat and fish was an excellent way of having food ready for serving when unexpected visitors arrived and so was much used in Inns. It would keep for some time if prepared carefully. It could be prepared at leisure and when the ingredients were at hand, put in a pot and covered with an airtight covering of clarified fat or butter: it would keep well provided the seal was not broken. which could make good use of a small boy's fishing. "And in the Spring they make them excellent Minnow tansies – for being washed well in salt, and their heads and tails cut off and their guts taken out, they prove excellent for that use, that is being fried with yolks of eggs, the flowers of cowslips and of primroses and a little tansy; thus used they make a dainty dish of Meat".

A Carp Pye

Take Carps and scald them, take out the great bones, pound the Carps in a stone Morter, pound some of the blood with the flesh which must be at the discretion of the Cook, because it must not be too soft, then lard it with the belly of a very fat Eele, season it, and bake it like red Deere and eat it cold.

It was commonly said that Lent was the season for salmon and sermons, and this was certainly so at the beginning of the century. Meat would not have been eaten in Lent or on Fridays so fish dishes were served instead. The Puritans felt this smacked of Popery and gradually their views gained ground.

Many large households farmed their own fish just as the Monasteries had before them. We know that the Paston family when building a house in Norfolk set out the gardens in three terraces down to the river where they made fish ponds. John Evelyn as quite a young man records doing exactly the same at the family home at Wotton: "I made the stews and receptacles for Fish". Unfortunately he does not tell us which kinds of fish were stocked. They would probably have been perch and pike and perhaps carp. There are very many recipes for carp in the cookery books of the time. Pike was described by Izaak Walton as "a freshwater wolf, a Tyrant" as it ate any other kind of fish it could in an open river, and so was not liked by fishermen. However, he liked it stuffed and said: "This dish of meat is too good for any but anglers, or very honest men".

The fish pond of a large house

Marinated Kippers

1 lb/450 g boned kippers
1 onion
4 sticks of celery
4 tablespoons of olive oil
2 tablespoons of wine vinegar
$1/2$ teaspoon salt
$1/2$ teaspoon mustard
Pepper
Squeezed garlic if liked.

Remove the skins from the kippers; if this is difficult then pour boiling water over them and lift off the skins, but do not cook. Cut them in finger-sized pieces and put in a dish. Finely slice the onion, put in a pan and bring to the boil, then drain at once. Cut celery into slices and sprinkle celery and onion over kippers. Whisk oil, vinegar and seasonings vigorously until they are emulsified and pour over the kippers. Leave to marinate, turning occasionally, for 4 hours.

Serve with a green salad of lettuce and watercress, and crisp French bread, or brown bread and butter

For nearly 20 years from about 1642 to 1661 Lent had not been observed by fasting owing to the Puritan influence and the rise of the Commonwealth party, though, no doubt, this varied from household to household. With the Restoration there was a revival of compulsory fasting in Lent. In one city butchers were forbidden to display meat for sale from Ash Wednesday until Good Friday, but for the sake of the aged and infirm people the magistrates granted licences to 3 butchers to sell meat during the first 3 weeks of Lent, and 5 others were allowed to sell during the following 3 weeks. In London the options seem to have been left open for when Pepys and a couple of friends dined at a tavern he records: "Sir Williams being unwilling to eat flesh, Captain Cocke and I had a breast of veal roasted". Perhaps Pepys did not wish to give up his Puritan ways, or maybe he liked his roast meat.

Of course, meat was less plentiful in the late winter and early spring. It is on record that "The Fishmongers' Company petitioned the King that Lent might be kept, because they had provided an abundance of fish for this season, and their prayer was granted". So there were vested interests at work as well as consciences.

To make dry Salmon Calvart in the boyling

Take a Gallon of Water, put to it a quart of Wine or Vinegar, Verjuice or four Beer, and a few sweet Herbs and Salt,and let your Liquor boyle extream fast, and hold your Salmon by the Tayle, and dip it in , and let it have a wawme, and so dip it in and out a dozen times, and that will make your Salmon Calvert, and so boyle it till it be tender.

The old recipe conjures up a lovely picture of the cook standing over her fish kettle of just boiling water holding her salmon by the tail and dipping it in again and again and letting it have "a warwme", till it be cooked. Of course, she was right because hard, fast boiling, or boiling for any length of time makes salmon hard and rather tasteless.

Centuries ago salmon was very plentiful and so was a cheap and ordinary dish – alas no longer. It is good served cold with mayonnaise but also delicious hot, cut into steaks, baked with butter and served with fried parsley. The crisp bright green parsley complements the pink lush flesh of the salmon. The trick with frying parsley is speed. Take springs of parsley from a big bunch (fresh, not limp) and if possible put them into a wire basket. Heat the deep frying oil until it smokes and the plunge the basket in for about 2 seconds, whip it out and turn the parsley onto kitchen paper for a minute to drain. Serve at once round the baked salmon.

Winchester from the east

Poached Salmon with Green Mayonnaise

3 lb/1.5 kg Salmon
1 onion
1 carrot
1 bay leaf
1 sprig of thyme
$1/2$ cup white wine
1 tablespoon salt
6 peppercorns

Wrap the salmon in a piece of cheesecloth, put all other ingredients and 3 pints of water in a fish kettle and simmer for 15 minutes. Put in the piece of salmon and bring to the boil; immediately lower the heat and simmer gently for 25 minutes covered. Leave in the liquid to cool, then drain it and unwrap it and remove the skin of the top-side ready for masking with the green mayonnaise.

1 cup spinach
$1/2$ cup watercress
$1/2$ cup parsley
$1/2$ cup tarragon
$1/4$ cup sour cream
1 cup homemade mayonnaise

Trim the greens of their stems and drop them into boiling water and boil for 5 minutes; turn into a sieve, cool under running water and squeeze dry. Put them into a blender with the sour cream and then mix into the mayonnaise. Mask the salmon with the green sauce and the remainder of the sauce serve in a sauceboat. Garnish with tomatoes and cucumber.

Celia Fiennes, the daughter of a Cromwellian colonel, on her journeys round England and into Scotland writes of how she bought for 9 pence, "which was full cheape enough", 2 pieces of salmon "halfe a one neer a yard long". But she did not proceed further into Scotland for, she writes, the Noblemen's houses:

are all kind of Castles and they live great, tho' in so nasty a way, as all things are, even in those houses, one has little stomack to eate or use any thing as I have been told by some that has travell'd there; and I am sure I mett with a sample of it enough to discourage my progress farther in Scotland – I attribute it wholly to their sloth for I see they sitt and do little – I think there were one or two at last did take spinning in hand at a lazy way; thence I tooke my fish to carry it to a place for the English to dress it.

Indeed, Celia Fiennes was not alone in her opinions for Sir John Perceval writes: "I ate in gloves for fear of the itch".

To drese a Dish of Hartichoaks

Take and boyle them in the Beef-pot, when they are tender sodden, take off the tops, leaving the bottoms with some ronnd about them, then put them into a Dish, put some fair water to them, two or three spoonfulls of Sack, a spoonfull of Sugar, and so let them boyle upon the coales, till pouring on the Liquor to give it a good tast, when they have boyled halfe an houre take the Liquor from them, and make ready some Cream boyled and thickned with the Yelk of an Egg or two, whole Mace, Salt, and Sugar with some lumps of Marrow, boyl it in the Cream, when it is boyled, put a good peice of sweet Butter in it, and toast some Toasts, and lay them under your Hartichoaks, and pour your cream and butter on them, Garnish it &c.

Christ College, Brecon, was originally a monastic school. It is beautifully situated on the edge of the town near the banks of the river Usk. In this river there was a plentiful supply of salmon, so much so that it had to be written into the school statutes that the boys should only be given salmon three times a week, and so they were saved from too great a monotony of diet.

At first sight it seems that the seventeenth-century diet must have been very dull and monotonous without so many of the flavours we have today like cocoa, coffee, tomatoes and green peppers, but their food changed with the seasons, and ours, with the advent of freezers, no longer does.

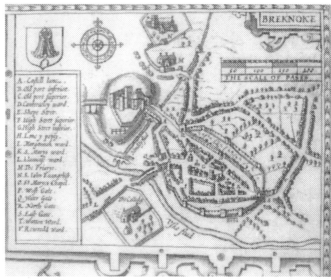

Seventeenth century Brecon

Salmon Cutlets
with Artichokes and Hollandaise Sauce

1 Cutlet of salmon per person

1 artichoke per person

2 tablespoons white wine or white wine vinegar

4 tablespoons water

2 egg yolks

4 oz/125 g butter

A little lemon juice

Salt and pepper

Boil the wine or vinegar and water together until they are reduced by two-thirds. Put them in a basin over hot water but never let the water boil or the sauce will get too hot and the eggs scramble. Stir in well-beaten yolks and add butter in small pieces, stirring all the time as the sauce thickens. Season to taste, take off the heat and slowly stir in the lemon juice. Serve in a sauceboat.

Butter a baking dish liberally and put in the salmon; put a little butter on top of each cutlet and then cover with foil. Bake in a moderate oven at 325°F (170°C) Gas Mark 3 for 10–15 minutes depending on the thickness of the cutlets. Put in a serving dish.

Boil the artichokes in salted water for half-an-hour, and arrange on the serving dish with the salmon; they make a good colour combination.

In the first three months of the year it was perhaps dull with salt meat and fish and many root vegetable stews and only the remaining apples and nuts.

Once spring came there were fresh herbs, sorrel and nettle tops which were greatly prized for cleansing the blood, new greens, fresh meat and chickens and then the excitement of the first dish of strawberries. These were followed in June by gooseberries and raspberries, the "thinnings" from the vegetable patch of carrots and beets, the little ones carefully pulled out to make way for their neighbours to grow big and fat. So on to cherries, early plums and gages, spinach, peas and beans, followed by apricots and late plums, mulberries, pears, apples, figs, grapes and artichokes. Finally in the Autumn came the vegetable crops for the winter use, beets, carrots, parsnips, turnips, swedes, garlic and onions, the last of the apples and pears, quinces and medlars all to be carefully stored or preserved.

The animals that could not be kept and fed throughout the winter were killed off one by one, and finally the pigs which had been fattened on acorns and beech mast in the forest were killed in late November and turned into black puddings and sausages to be eaten before Christmas, sides of bacon were salted and hams hung in the chimney to smoke, and fat clarified ready for the first lean months of the coming year. Bread and dripping, suet puddings and dumplings in the stews all helped to keep out the winter cold while waiting for spring to come again.

To dresse Soales

Take a pair of Soales, Lard them through with watred fresh Salmon, then lay your Soales on a Table, or Pye-plate, cut your Salmon, lard all of an equall length one each side, and leave the Lard but short, then floure the Soales, and fry them in the best Ale you can get, when they are fryed, lay them on a warm Pye-plate, and so serve them to the Table with a Sallet dish full of Anchovey Sauce, and three or four Oranges.

Eating for pleasure rather than for survival was a matter of skill and ingenuity on the part of the cook in the seventeenth century. Visitors from abroad remarked with surprise at how well the people ate in England, that food was good and plentiful, but careful cooking and good presentation was all important. Samuel Pepys notes in his diary for 15 January 1663 that he and his wife were invited to supper with Admiral, Sir William Penn, father of the founder of Pennsylvannia, "My wife and I to see Sir William Penn and there supped with him much against my stomach, for the dishes were so deadly foule that I could not endure to look upon them". So it was cooking and presentation more than money, and no doubt, fine table silver that mattered.

Elizabeth Pepys

Dover Sole with Herbs

Fillets of Dover or Lemon sole, or plaice
3 oz/75 g butter
Salt and pepper
2 tablespoons chopped sorrel leaves
2 tablespoons chopped fennel
1 tablespoon chopped fennel
2 lemons

Ask the fishmonger to prepare the fish into fillets for you

Chop the herbs leaving some of the fennel on one side for decorating the dish just before serving as this gives a brighter green colour.

Melt the butter in a large frying pan and put in the fish; sprinkle with salt and pepper and add the herbs and the juice of one lemon. Cook for a few minutes and then carefully turn the fish over; stir in the herbs. When the fillets are just cooked put them on the serving dish and cover with the herbs and juices. Sprinkle over the uncooked chopped fennel and serve immediately with slices of the second lemon.

Without a good deal of help food must have looked a rather uniform grey when flour was pale brown unless it had been sieved and forced through linen to get it more or less white as we know it today. Small wonder that they loved to use colourful ingredients like saffron and oranges and lemons, to cheer up dishes.

Pepys also tells us that soon after they moved to a larger house in London his wife did some baking in her new kitchen: "So home to dinner, where I found my wife making of pies and tarts to try her oven with, which she had never done yet, but not knowing the nature of it, did heat it too hot and so a little overbake her things, but knows how to do better another time". The cook learnt by trial and error.

By the time that Mrs Pepys was cooking in London most of the fuel used would have been coal brought by water into the city. Elsewhere in the country wood was the main fuel for England was rich in forests. Logs and faggots, twigs made into bundles and tied together, would be burnt in most hearths though peat was used where it could be dug locally. People had to use what was to hand and one traveller wrote how she saw all round Peterborough cow dung plastered up on the walls of the houses to dry into cakes, and she remarked "its a very offensive fewell".

To Dress Flounders or Playce with Garlick and Mustard

Take Flounders very new, and cut all the Fins and Tailes, then take out the Gutts and wipe them very clean, they must not be at all washt, then with you Knife scotch them on both sides very grosely, then take the tops of Time and cut them very small, and take a little Salt, Mace, and Nutmeg, and mingle the Time and them together, and season the Flounders, then lay them on the Grid-iron and bast them with Oyle or Butter, let not the fire be too hot, when that side next the fire is brown, turn it, and when you turn it, bast it on both sides till you have boyld them Brown, when they are enough make your Sauce with Mustard two or three Spoonful according to discretion, six Anchoves dissolved very well, about half a pound of butter drawn up with garlick, vinegar, or bruised garlick in other vinegar rubb the bottom of your dish with garlick. So put your sauce to them, and serve them, you may fry them if you please.

Bess of Hardwick, Countess of Shrewsbury, was an old lady when she built Hardwick Hall on a hill in Derbyshire; 4 times widowed and 4 times heiress. When the house was finished and furnished in 1601 she had an inventory made of what was in it and in which room so we have a perfect picture of how this house looked and what it contained. It is clear from the inventory that textiles such as tapestry wall hangings, curtains, bed curtains and coverlets, table cloths and cushions were a major part of the decoration at Hardwick and that they gave colour and warmth to this great house with its enormous windows;

Hardwick Hall
More glass than wall

The Countess must have felt the cold for she had window curtains in her room of warm red cloth which were supplemented by "three coverlets to hang before a windowe", and another coverlet to hang before a door, and there was a "counterpoynt of tapestrie to hang before an other doore", and tapestries covered the walls. Her bed was a large four poster with curtains of "scarlet" which was a fine woollen cloth rather than the more opulent silk hangings seen in the guest bedrooms. Her bed curtains were trimmed richly with silver and gold lace, with a gold fringe and red silk buttons and loops. The bed also had an additional set of curtains of purple "bays" for extra warmth in the winter. For her bed the Countess had a mattress, a featherbed, a bolster, a pillow, two little pillows, two quilts covered with linen, three pairs of fustian blankets which had a linen warp and a cotton weft, and six woollen blankets from Catalonia. On the floor around the bed were 8 fledges which were mats made by quilting feathers between two layers of material.

Her maid who slept in an adjoining chamber had "a mattress, a featherbed, a bolster, a blanket and two coverlets". In "a little room was the Close stoole (containing a chamber pot) with blewe cloth stitch with white, red and black silk fringe, three pewter basins".

Hake with Ratatouille

Cutlets of Hake, one per person
2 oz/50 g butter
1 clove garlic, crushed
1 bay leaf
Salt and pepper
2 medium onions
5 or 6 tomatoes
6 medium courgettes
butter for frying

Melt the butter in an ovenproof dish and place in it the hake cutlets, crushed garlic and bay leaf and sprinkle with salt and pepper. Cover and put in the oven at 375°F (180°C) Gas Mark 4 for about 25 minutes.

Melt some butter in a frying pan and fry sliced onions till just brown, put in a dish to keep warm. Slice courgettes and fry them until they are quite brown, add them to the onions. Slice the tomatoes in quarters and add them as well, stir all together so that they are well mixed, cover and put in the oven with the fish for the last 10 minutes so that they are really hot.

Take fish out of the oven and remove the skin and put it on a serving dish, pour juices from the pan over it. Surround the fish with the ratatouille.

The other furniture in the Countess's bedroom consisted of a high joint stool, 2 joint stools, a Cupboard, a folding table, a chair of "russet satten stript with silver", 2 embroidered foot stools, 6 religious books, an hour glass, a looking glass and 2 brushes.

There were also 4 great "trunckes" and several other chests, coffers and boxes, which presumably contained her clothes and other personal items as this was before the advent of chests of drawers and so everything had to be packed into wooden chests.

Oak coffer at Castle Rising

To roast a Pike

Take a Pike, scour off the slime, take out the Entralls, Lard it with the backs of Pickled Herrings, you must have a sharp Bodkin to make the holes, no Larding Pins will go thorow, then take some great Oysters, Claret Wine, season it with Pepper, Salt, and Nutmeg, stuff the belly of the Pike with these Oysters, intermix with them Rosemary, Tyme, Winter-Savory, Sweet Marjorum, a little Onyon and Garlick, sow these in the belly of the Pike, prepare two sticks about the breadth of a Lath, these two sticks and the Spit must be as broad as the Pike being tyed on the Spit, tye the Pike on, winding Pack-threed about the Pike along, but there must be tyed by the pack-thread all along the side of the pike which is not defended by the spit, and the Lathes, Rosemary and Bayes, bast the pike with Butter and Clarret Wine, with some Anchoves dissolved in it, when it is wasted rip up the belly of the Pike, and the Oysters will be the same, but the herbs which are whole must be taken out.

Bess of Hardwick would probably have had meals served in the little dining chamber when she was not entertaining, and only eating with her granddaughter Lady Arabella Stuart, and other members of her household. There was "In the dyning Chamber a long drawing table, a turkey Carpet for it, a Chair of turkie worke, a stool of turkie work, fowtene Joyed stools, a fyre shovell, a payre of tongues". The Turkey carpet was a heavy tablecloth used on the table in between meals which would have given colour and a feeling of warmth to this rather sparsely furnished room. The chair and stool of Turkey work would have been padded and covered with needlework in wool, and the joined stools were of solid oak. At this date there were seldom carpets on the floor though there was one in the Chapel at Hardwick.

In the inventory there are $2^{1}/2$ closely printed pages listing the linen of the household. Some of this was in lengths and not made up, such as "a piece of diaper for napkins rowde with blew, 41 yardes long", and "a piece of fyne newe damask for table clothes of too yards and a quarter brode, and seventene yardes three quarters long". In one trunk there were 34 sheets 16 pillowcases and "a sweetbag of chaungeable taffetie" and a "cubberd cloth" on the top, presumably as a dust cover. The sweet bag was a little bag with a drawstring top, filled with dried lavender, or dried sweet herbs, to scent the linen in the trunk; changeable taffeta was shot taffeta. There were many more descriptions of grander items such as a pair of pillowcases "trymmed with a great gold lace" and six pillowcases "trymmed with gold and silk lace".

Tuna-Fish Pie

7 oz/200 g tin of tuna fish
1/2 pint/275 ml milk
1 tablespoon butter
1 tablespoon plain flour
6 oz/175 g sweetcorn
1/2 teaspoon thyme
Freshly ground pepper

Shortcrust Pastry

8 oz/225 g flour
4 oz/125 g lard, or lard and margarine
Cold water to mix

Melt the butter in a saucepan and stir in the flour and cook stirring all the time for 2 minutes. Take off the heat and gradually add the milk beating it into the flour and butter until it is smooth, return to the heat and bring up to the boil so that it thickens. Add flaked tuna fish and sweetcorn and thyme and pepper. Put it into a buttered baking-dish.

Mix up pastry and roll out on a floured board. Damp the edges of the pie dish and place the pastry over, trim the edges and press well down; decorate with any left over pastry, make two holes in the top for steam to come out, and brush with milk. Bake in a hot oven 450°F (230°C) Gas Mark 8 for about 25 minutes.

In the Porter's Lodge there was a bed and bedding, and here was kept the vast amount of family gold and silver, all carefully listed giving a description and the weight of each piece. It begins with "A Cupp of Angle golde with a Cover saying sixtene ounces and a quater; a Cupp of french Crowne gold with a Cover, waying nyne ounces and three quarters" down to the last items "an oystridge egg trymmed with silver and guilt with a cover not wayed, a Currall Rock, Eight stone Jugges trymmed with silver and guilt not wayed, a tosting forke of wood, trymmed with silver".

So the inventory goes on giving details and making it clear that this is an extraordinary house built and furnished by an extraordinary woman. Both Bess of Hardwick and Hardwick Hall were legends in their time and have been down the centuries.

Sweet bag

To marine Carps, Mullet, Gornet, Rochet, or Wale, &c

Take a quart of water to a Gallon of Vinegar, a good handfull of Bay-leaves, as much Rosemary, a quarter of a pound of Pepper beaten, put all these together, and let it seeth softly, and season it with a little Salt, then fry your Fish with frying Oyle till it be enough, then put in an earthen Vessell, and lay the Bay-leaves and Rosemary between and about the Fish, and pour the Broath upon it, and when it is cold cover it, &c

The great seventeenth-century house would have large kitchen quarters; nearly half the ground floor of Hardwick Hall was used in this way. Next to the Hall was the Buttery and beyond that the very large kitchen. The scullery was placed so that it could be entered from both the Buttery and from the kitchen so that dirty plates and dishes from the Hall and pots from the kitchen could be taken straight there for washing. Shakespeare wrote "Greasy Joan doth keel the pot", and poor greasy Joan must have had a dreadful job in the days when there was no detergent or even soap.

Beyond the kitchen were more rooms and outhouses each with their separate use. There was a dry larder, and a wet larder for raw meat with hooks in the beams from which to hang carcasses, a pastry room and a bake house, a stillroom for making up and keeping medicines, a scouring house, laundry and linen room. In even more modest country houses and farms there would be a dairy and a cheese room, a brewhouse with a malthouse and a hophouse, and beyond that perhaps a fish house and a slaughterhouse. Under the house would be cellars containing not only ale, beer, wine and many home-made drinks like mead and hippocras but food carefully preserved and stored. Barrels of varying sizes containing salted fish and meat and more exotic things like capers imported from abroad, or broom buds gathered locally and pickled as a substitute for capers.

Each generation learnt from the last the art of preserving food for it was vitally important for the supply of food through a long winter. The methods of salting, potting, conserving, candying, brewing and distilling were carefully noted and passed on.

Experiments were tried out on how to keep food in good condition for the longest time and this became increasingly important as voyages became longer and ships ventured further and further into unknown waters.

Casseroled Fish

Any firm white fish will be suitable

1 portion of fish per person

2 tablespoons olive oil

2 cloves of garlic

4 large tomatoes

1/2 teaspoon of thyme or chopped dill

1 glass of white wine

Salt and pepper

Parsley, if liked

Cut the fish into about 2 inch pieces. Heat the olive oil in a casserole and then add the fish; sauté gently over a low heat for a few minutes turning it carefully so that it does not stick. Cut up tomatoes. Add the rest of the ingredients and cover the casserole; simmer gently for about 20 minutes so that the tomatoes are reduced to a sauce. Add a tablespoonful of chopped parsley if liked, and then serve.

Kitchen at St. Fagans Castle, Cardiff

FISH

To dress Soales another way

Take Soales, fry them half enough, then take Wine seasoned with Salt, grated Ginger, and a little Garlick, let the Wine and seasoning boyl in a Dish, when that boyles and your Soales are half fry'd, take the Soales and put them into the Wine, when they are sufficiently stewed upon their backs, lay the two halfs open on the one side and on the other, then lay Anchoves finely washed all along, and on the Anchoves slices of Butter, turn the two sides over again, let them stew till they be ready to be eaten, then take them out, lay them on the Dish, pour some of the clear Liquor which they stew in upon them, and squeeze an Orange in.

Cooks in large households needed not only knowledge of food and skill but also considerable strength unless they had "lusty servants" to carry carcasses, lift down heavy iron spits which were usually stored above the chimney breast, carry large cauldrons, or hold very long handled frying pans over the fire. There are mentioned "leather aproned cooks", and these aprons would have given protection from the heat of the fire and sparks as well as from spilt food.

Cottagers might still have been cooking in one large pot over a fire in the hearth, but most households would have had more sophisticated appliances like the chimney crane. This was used for holding cooking pots over the fire. The crane would be swung over the fire and then pulled back to the side so that the cook could attend to the cooking pot without bending over the fire. The pots could be raised or lowered by means of a long handle on the crane.

Spits were used for roasting large joints in front of the fire and would have a drip tray underneath. The spit had to be turned to prevent the meat from burning on the side nearest the fire. This was usually a job for the young or for the elderly, or little dogs running in a wheel, and later became more mechanized. Birds spits were made of much thinner rods to go through the birds. Basket spits were made like an iron cage for small joints that it was better not to pierce with an ordinary spit, and fish that would fall apart as it cooked, could be held safely. They were made with a hinge for easy access.

Salamanders, flat and rather like a shovel, were put in the fire to get red hot and then held over a dish to cook, or brown the top.

Wafering irons, like a waffle iron, were used to make wafer breads out of a sweet batter, and these were rolled into cones and filled with cream. It was a custom for them to be made on Mothering Sunday in mid-Lent so that young people working away from home could take some as a present to their mothers on this Sunday.

Fish and Capers in Black Butter

Any fish with a sturdy texture such as cod, halibut or fresh haddock can be used for this recipe

> 1 portion of fish per person
> 1/4 lb/125 g butter
> 1 tablespoon of capers
> 1 small onion
> 2 bay leaves
> Vinegar
> Pinch of thyme
> 1 tablespoon chopped parsley

Put the fish in a wide pan with the onion, sliced, and the thyme and bay leaves. Add enough water to just cover the fish and a little salt. Slowly bring to the boil and then very gently simmer until the fish is firm and cooked. Carefully take it out and drain before putting on a serving dish, then keep warm.

Melt the butter until it is dark brown, do this slowly; meanwhile scatter the capers and parsley over the fish and pour over the brown butter.

Quickly put 2 tablespoons of vinegar into the hot pan, swish it round and pour over the fish, serve at once.

Bakestone or griddle

MEAT

To bake Brawn

Take two Buttocks and hang them up two or three dayes, then take them down and dip them into hot Water, and pluck off the skin, dry them very well with a clean Cloth, when you have so done, take Lard, cut it in peeces as big as your little finger, and season it very well with Pepper, Cloves, Mace, Nutmeg, and Salt, put each of them into an earthen pot, put in a Pint of Clarret wine, a pound of Mutton Suet. So close it with Past, let the Oven be well heated, and so bake them, you must give them time for the baking according to the bigness of the Haunches, and the thickness of the Pots, they commonly allot seaven hours for the baking of them, let them stand three dayes, then take off their Cover, and poure away all the Liquor, then have clarified Butter, and fill up both the Pots to keep it for the use, it will very well keep two or three moneths.

The Frenchman Henri Misson de Valbourg wrote about his travels in England and was astonished by the heavy consumption of fish and meat; this was not confined to the gentry but included large numbers of the middle-class. The farm labourer did not have butcher's meat but usually had his own pig annually, and rabbits and hens. At the taverns in London men breakfasted on salt fish, anchovies or dried herrings with bread and ale. Misson de Valbourg describes the scene at dinner time:

Generally four spits, one over another, carry round each five or six pieces of Butcher's Meat, Beef, Mutton, Veal, Pork, Lamb; you have what quantity you please cut off, fat, lean, much or little done; with this, a little salt and Mustard upon the side of a Plate, a bottle of Beer and a roll; and there is your Feast.

This dinner would have cost a shilling or a little more which would have been a peasant's daily wage.

The written records certainly emphasize the meat courses served and vegetables are not so often mentioned; country people must have grown and eaten far more than Londoners. Peas and beans were grown and dried for winter use. Certainly visitors from abroad were impressed by the plenteousness of the country. Defoe tells us

Pewter plates and meat forks

38

Roast Buttock of Beef

3 lb/1.350 g beef topside or fillet rolled

Pastry

8 oz/225 g flour

4 oz/100 g lard

Mushroom sauce

1/2 lb/225 g mushrooms

1/4 pint/150 ml milk

1 heaped teaspoon butter

1 heaped teaspoon flour

Plenty of freshly ground black pepper

Put the joint in a roasting tin with a little dripping and place in a pre-heated oven at 425°F (220°C) Gas Mark 7 for 15 minutes and then reduce the heat to 375°F (190°C) Gas Mark 5 and cook for a further 40 minutes.

Meanwhile make up the pastry, fairly stiff, and leave in the fridge.

Put the sliced mushrooms in a pan with the milk and pepper and a little salt and cook gently until they are soft.

Roll out the pastry on a floured board. Take the meat out of the oven and remove any string or fat. Pour off any excess fat in the roasting tin. Completely encase the meat in the pastry and brush with milk. Put it back in the tin and replace in the oven for a further 20 minutes.

Put the butter in a pan and melt, then add the flour and cook for 2 minutes before adding the milk from the mushrooms slowly beating all the time until it is a smooth thick sauce, finally add in the mushrooms and keep the sauce warm to serve with the beef.

Remove the beef onto a serving dish and make gravy as usual; serve with potatoes and a green vegetable like calabrese.

that as he stood on Bushey Heath with 2 foreign visitors looking at the rolling countryside spread out before them they said in wonder: "England was not like other's countrys, but it was all a planted garden". Except in large cities all houses and cottages had gardens and quite big ones including vegetable gardens, if possible

walled so as to keep rabbits out and fruit trees grown up the walls, and large orchards. Fruit was enjoyed and was sometimes given as a very acceptable gift; the more exotic the better. We know that at least a dozen varieties of peaches and two of nectarines were grown at this period.

Sugar was expensive and only gradually replaced honey in many recipes which catered for those who enjoyed sweet things. In 1644 Lionel Playters, Rector of Uggeshall, was one of the Royalist parsons ejected from his living by the Earl of Manchester's Committee for Scandalous Ministers. Among other things he was accused of spending the day of 31 August "drinking with a papist and armourer, since gone to the royal army". But the prime cause of his ejection was "his Eating Custard after a scandalous manner"; apparently he liberally added sack to it and ate it with great greediness. He survived and held his living again after the Restoration for the rest of his life.

To boile a rump of Beef after the French fashion

Take a rump of Beef, or the little end of the Brisket, and perboile it halfe an houre, then take it up and put it in a deep Dish then slash it in the side that the gravy may come out, then throw a little Pepper and Salt between every cut, then fill up the Dish with the best Clarret wine, and put to it three or foure peeces of large Mace and set it on the coales close covered, and boyle it above an houre and a halfe, but turn it often in the meantime, then with a spoone take off the fatt and fill it with Clarret wine, and slice six Onyons , and a handfull of Capers or Broom budds, halfe a dozen of hard Lettice sliced, three spoonfuls of wine Vinegar and as much verjuce, and then set it a boyling with these things in it till, it be tender, and serve it up with brown Bread and Sippets fryed with Butter, but be sure there be not too much fatt in it, when you serve it.

In his *Boke of Nurture* John Russell gives a chapter on the "Kervying of flesh" and another on the "Kervying of fische" and shows that there were set rules and conventions about carving. The carver in a royal or noble household was often a knight, and before the introduction of the fork had to have considerable skill and a good knowledge of anatomy. He might not touch venison with his hand but having sliced the piece deftly he put the best piece on his lord's plate using his broad-bladed carving knife. Birds he might lift by their legs with his left hand before dismembering them. He could recourse to a spoon but the really accomplished carver seldom did.

Pepys Library

Carbonnade of Beef

2 lb/900 g steak

8 tablespoons flour

3 teaspoons salt, and a little pepper

2 oz/50 g dripping

1 lb/450 g onions, sliced

3/4 pint/425 ml beer

2 cloves garlic

Bouquet garni

1 teaspoon sugar

2 tablespoons vinegar

Cut the steak in slices about 1/2 inch thick and 3 inches square. Coat them well in flour, salt and pepper. Fry the meat in the dripping until brown. Transfer to the casserole and fry the onions. Add the rest of the flour and stir well. Pour the beer into the frying-pan and stir until it boils. Pour over the meat and add the garlic, bouquet garni, and sugar. Cover and cook slowly for 2 1/2 – 3 hours. Add the vinegar just before serving.

This book printed by Wynkyn de Worde, Caxton's successor, gave a list of carving terms – so you "break a deer, rear a goose, lift a swan, spoyle a hen, disfigure a peacock, allay a pheasant, thigh a pigeon, unjoint a bittern, chine a salmon, splatt a pike, splay a bream, side a haddock, culpon a trout, barbe a lobster" and so on; he ends the list saying "Here endith the goodly terms". These fantastic terms continued throughout the Tudor and Stuart times and are also found in Robert May's *Accomplished Cook*.

When the household was not worthy of a carver then the lady of the house carved and young ladies had to learn the art. As late as the 1830s and 1840s there was a flourishing school of carving in London where a young lady before her marriage could attend a course of 12 lessons at a guinea a lesson, exclusive of the cost of the dishes upon which she operated. So the man of the house carving is quite a recent innovation.

So too is the formal dinner party as we know it with an equal number of ladies and gentlemen sitting round the table alternately; this is only about a hundred years old. Before this the host would lead in the most important lady present having asked the most important gentlemen to take his wife in. The rest of the guests followed into the dining room in a haphazard fashion and if 2 or 3 gentlemen were in the middle of a discussion then they would all go in together and sit together so as to continue it as there was no idea of an arranged table. Pepys gave a dinner party for 11 people and hired a cook, a man, for the occasion.

To Sauce a Pig

Take a faire large Pig and cut off his Head, then slit him thorow the midst, then take forth his Bones, then lay him in warm water one night, then Collar him up like Brawn; then boile him tender in fair water, and when he is boyled put him into a Earthen Pot or Pan into Water and Salt, for that will make him white, and season the flesh, for you must not put Salt in the boyling for that will make it black, then take a quart of the same Broth, and a quart of white Wine, boyle them together to make some drink for it, put into it two or three Bay leaves, when it is cold uncloath the Pig, and put it into the same drink, and it will continue a quarter of a year. It is a necessary Dish in any Gentlemans House, when you serve it in, serve it with green Fennel, as you do Sturgeon with Vinegar in Saucers.

Let workman at night bring in wood, or a log,
Let none come home empty, but slut and thy dog.

So wrote Farmer Tussor in the sixteenth century and indeed it must have been a very good rule that all the workmen, children and other members of the family did not come home empty handed but collected wood along the way. The household fire that was for warmth, cooking and hot water was kept in day and night all the year round, and must have consumed an enormous amount of fuel.

The country workmen had rights of mesyrd; that is certain rights to certain wood. He might not cut any wood, but he might take out any dead wood "by hook or by crook". The agricultural labourer had an implement called a hook which he used mainly for weeding rather like a modern walking stick, or golf club, but the right-angled piece did the weeding. The crook, of course, belonged to the shepherds. So the workers, not vagrants, were legally allowed in the forests to pull out any dead wood from the trees themselves or from the undergrowth, and use it for their fires. This helped to keep the forests tidy as well as supply tenants with a necessity of life.

The right of mesyrd went hand in hand with the right of pannage which was swine feeding in the forests in the autumn on acorns and beech mast. The swineherd could collect fallen timber or drag dead branches out of the trees while keeping an eye on the pigs. Sticks would be collected and tied neatly into bundles known as faggots.

Wood, owing to its grain which makes thousands of channels up through each stick or branch, burns very fast when upright, and much more slowly when horizontal. Faggots would be placed upright like a wigwam when quick heat was required and put flat when a long-lasting steady heat was wanted. A good blaze would be wanted to start off a big joint roasting on a spit and then a steady heat for a couple of hours. Birds and fish needed a good heat for a much shorter time and we have seen how they were put into little ironwork cages on a spit so that they would not fall apart.

Cooks needed to learn how to control their fires by using their fuels intelligently and also needed to know their chimneys. No doubt the fire would draw better and burn faster if the wind was in a certain direction, or the door shut or open.

Pork with Apples and Sage

6 lean slices of pork
1 lb/450 g cooking apples
1 lb/450 g onions
1/2 pint/275 ml stock
2 sage leaves
salt and pepper
2 tablespoons flour

Mix flour seasoning and sage finely chopped and coat the pork slices. Heat some oil in a frying pan and lightly fry the pork. Remove to a fireproof dish or casserole. Fry the onions and meanwhile peel and chop up the apples. Put cooked onions into the casserole and cover all with the stock. Cover casserole and put in the oven at 325°F (170°C) Gas Mark 3 for 45 minutes. Take out and taste; adjust seasoning if necessary. Serve with chick peas to which a few chopped tomatoes have been added a few minutes before serving.

Casket showing figures of the elements

To dry Neats Tongues

Take Bay Salt beaten very fine, and Salt-Peter of each a like and rub your Tongues very well with that, and cover all over with it, and as it wasts put on more, and when they are very hard and stiffe, they are enough, then rowle them in Bran, and dry them before a soft fire, and before you boyle them, let them lye one night in Pumpe Water, and boyle them in the same sort of water.

Wild pigs have been in Britain since Neolithic times and, being scavengers, have been easy to domesticate. Their bones have been found on most Roman sites and a Roman coin of A.D.140 shows a side view of a sow with 6 sucking piglets, presumably half her litter. Medieval illustrations shown the British pig to be long-legged, hairy and with rather a long snout. Pigs remained small until recent breeding for larger animals. The shoulders are now smaller and the hindquarters much bigger. Pigs in the wild will eat worms, slugs and insects and also enjoy fruit and fungi – a fact that was later exploited when they were trained to locate and rout out truffles. They also like nuts, beech mast and acorns.

Oak forests have predominated in Britain since about 5000 B.C. and early illustrations show swineherds knocking down acorns from the trees for their pigs to eat. This was a task for November when the acorns were ripe and the pigs were being fattened up for killing in December. They could not all be fed through the winter and so pregnant sows were kept and the old boar, his job done, provided the Boar's Head at the Christmas feast.

The pig was cut up and much of it preserved by either salting or pickling and smoking so that it would last for months. The Romans used the dry cure method of rubbing salt into the meat repeatedly and so today we have bacon. A side of the pig's back, without the legs, was known by the Saxon term "flitch". This was often very fat but was popular until the nineteenth century. A small piece would make a meal for a large peasant family when boiled with root vegetables and dried beans or pearl barley. It was extensively used on board ship on long voyages.

The legs were cured by being put into pickle for about 3 weeks and then smoked. This was originally done over a small fire out of doors, but later chimneys in farm houses were built with smoke holes, and bacon racks at the back; sometimes these have been mistaken for priest holes. The meat would hang up in the smoke out of the reach of dogs and flies. The type of wood burnt on the fire would give a distinctive flavour to the ham; oak was the most popular, pine would give a resinous taste.

Baked Ham with Apples

3 lb/1.35 kg Ham or Gammon
3 medium cooking apples
3 oz/75 g raisins
1 cup of cider

Parboil the joint of ham by putting it in a pan and covering it with cold water. Bring to the boil and turn down the heat so that it simmers gently for 30 minutes.

Cut the apples across the middle and scoop out the cores. Stuff them with raisins and put them back together in pairs.

Grease a roasting tin and put the parboiled ham in it with the apples.

Bake in a pre-heated oven at 375°F (190°C) Gas Mark 5 for a further 50 minutes.

Put the ham on a serving dish; divide the apples carefully and place them round the joint; keep it warm. Make gravy as usual and add a cupful of cider if liked.

Cottage Kitchen

A Persian Dish

Take the fleshy part of a Leg of Mutton stript from the fat and sinews, beat that well in a Morter with Pepper, and salt, and a little Onyon or Garlick water by it self or with hearbs according to your tast, then make it up in flat cakes and let them be kept twelve houres between two Dishes before you use them, then fry them with butter in a frying pan and serve them with the same butter, and you will finde it a Dish of savoury meat.

Often medieval houses and castles had separate kitchen buildings which seemed to burn down regularly. With the building of stone and brick chimneys the fire risk was reduced, but still was a major hazard. It was bound to be with so many open fires, timber-framed houses and thatched roofs.

It is recorded that in 1653 a fire broke out in Marlborough which spread very rapidly and nearly all the houses burnt down leaving about 1,500 people homeless. These were no insurance arrangements and so the homeless had to depend on charity. This was forthcoming from the citizens of Bristol who were very sympathetic and raised £227. This was taken to Marlbrough by the Chamberlain, the Swordbearer and a sargeant whose expenses for the three day return journey amounted to £2.18.6 and this included 6/- "for a portmantle and pillion to carry the money".

The Great Fire of London as Pepys might have seen it

Roast Lamb with White Beans

1 leg of lamb

1 lb/450 g white beans

2 cloves of garlic

4 tomatoes

2 onions

1 tablespoon rosemary

Soak the beans overnight in plenty of water.

Cut the cloves of garlic lengthways and insert near the bone at each end of the leg of lamb and trim off excess fat. Melt a little butter in a roasting tin and put in joint and dust with fresh pepper. Roast as usual according to weight.

Drain water from the beans and cover them with boiling salted water, add the two onions and a bouquet garni. Cook slowly, about half an hour, till they are tender but still firm. In another pan melt a lump of butter, add onions and tomatoes cut up and the rosemary. Cook down to a purée and then gently stir in the beans so as not to break them, simmer to heat through the beans and serve.

The Great Fire of London, 1666, started at a baker's in Pudding Lane, and the flames, driven by an east wind, leapt across the narrow lanes and devoured street after street of old wooden houses. The fire raged for 5 days, and the King and his brother ordered sailors to blow up whole streets to create wide gaps which the fire could not cross. There are eye witness accounts of this terrifying fire, and people fleeing before it with the soles of their shoes burning through. Samuel Pepys piled many of his belongings and silver into a cart, and still in his nightgown, drove it to a friend's house for safe-keeping. Then back home he dug a pit in his garden and put in his wine and Parmesan cheese and covered them up hoping to save them from the fire. He took his wife and maid and his gold, worth about £2,350, by boat down the river to Woolwich. He saw the warehouses full of tar, pitch and oil all buring fiercely; "and saw how horribly the sky looks, all on fire in the night, was enough to put us out of our wits; and indeed, it was extremely dreadful, for it looks as if it was at us, and the whole heaven on fire".

More than 100,000 people were made homeless, but with great speed food was brought in from the country, and within a week both Christopher Wren and John Evelyn submitted plans for the rebuilding of the city. Many citizens were ruined but most of them managed to rebuild their homes and businesses. Christopher Wren moved to a house on the south bank of the Thames, which is still there, and from it he could watch the progress of the building of the new St. Paul's Cathedral.

To boyle Pigeons

Stuffe the Pigeons with Parsley, and Butter, and put them into an Earthen Pot, and put some sweet Butter to them and let them boyle, take Parsley, Time, and Rosemary, chop them and put them to them; take some sweet Butter and put in withall some Spinages, take a little gross Pepper and Salt, and season it withall, then take the yelk of an Egge and strain it with Verjuice, and put to them, lay Sippets in the Dish and serve it.

Pigeons were one of the few forms of fresh meat to be had in winter in medieval times. The Romans had encouraged them to nest by building earthenware turrets on the roofs of their houses. Later it was the Lord of the Manor who had a dovecot, and also had the power to license other gentry to have one so that there would probably be 2 to a parish. Gradually this was relaxed and farmers and even cottagers would have a pigeon loft built into a barn or cottage roof. Some church towers were also fitted with wooden nesting-boxes up until the end of the last century so that the parson of the parish could keep pigeons for his table. As the birds are greedy and have a very strong homing instinct they are easy to tame, but they do plunder the farmers' cornfields and this was often a source of friction.

They were also kept by people living in towns and we know that Pepys kept them in London, just a sufficient number for his own household. He writes about how sad it was to see them at the time of the great fire of London when it had been raging for days: "Among other things, the poor pigeons, I perceive, were loth to leave their houses, but hovered about the windows and balconys till they were some of them burned, their wings, and fell down".

The pigeons to be found in London now do not make good eating; they are rock pigeons who have happily taken to city life. It is the wood pigeons living in the country on the fat of the land that are delicious if correctly cooked. If they are young with pink supple legs and feet then they can be fried or roasted. If they are older then they are better casseroled or put in a pie with other meat such as steak and kidney, or ham or bacon, and some wine otherwise the meat can be rather tough and dry.

Mrs Beeton ends her recipe for pigeon pie with the direction: "Have ready a few of the pigeons' feet, scalded and the toes cut off. Before serving replace the pastry ornament in the centre with the feet, fixing them in a nearly upright position. The pie may be served either hot or cold". She recommended this as a means of identification which certainly might have been necessary at a large lunch or supper party.

Pigeon and Steak Casserole

2 pigeons, fresh or frozen (thawed)
1 lb/450 g stewing steak
1/4 lb/125 g kidney
1 onion
2 sticks celery
1 carrot
salt and pepper
1/2 teaspoon mixed herbs

Gently fry the onions until brown and put them in the bottom of the casserole. Fry the pigeons and put them in the centre of the casserole. Mix the herbs with a little flour and coat the meat; fry it quickly and put it in the casserole round the birds. Slice the celery and carrot and put in, adding enough water to come half-way up the casserole nearly covering the birds.

Put in a moderate oven at 350°F (180°C) Gas Mark 4 for 2 1/2 hours.

Taste and adjust seasoning if necessary and thicken gravy if liked. To give it a more gamey flavour add a small glass of brandy, and serve with redcurrant jelly.

Small dovecot above granary, Elsworth

To Pot Venison

Take a haunch of Venison not hunted, and bone it, then take three ounces of Pepper beaten, twelve Nutmegs, with a handful of Salt, and mince them together with Wine Vinegar, then wet your Venison with Wine Vinegar and season it, then with a Knife make holes on the lean sides of the Hanch, and stuff it as you would stuff Beef with Parsley, then put it into the Pot with the fat side downward then clarifie three pound of Butter, and put it thereon, and past upon the Pot, and let it stand in the Oven five or six hours, then take it out, and with a vent press it down to the bottom of the Pot, and let it stand till it be cold, then take the Gravy of the top of the Pot and melt it, and boyle it half away and more, then put it in again with the Butter on the top of the Pot.

In his "affectionate portrait" of the dovecots of Cambridgeshire, Peter Jeevar tells how pigeon houses and dovecots were the predecessors of todays' broilerhouses, but the inmates could fly free and feed themselves by day and just come home to roost. It was pigeon farming with regular management; the old birds being culled from time to time and some of the young birds, or squabs as they are called, being taken as well so as to keep the number down. A dovecot would be built to house a certain number of breeding pairs. Some of the great houses with large households and many staff to feed would have a large dovecot able to house thousands of birds.

Some dovecots were built for manor houses like the one at Haslingfield which stands in the field just outside the garden and moat. It is circular and built of soft red brick with a 3 course plat band and a decorative cornice. It has a conical roof with fish scale tiles rising to an 8 posted cupola and is indeed very handsome. It is a pretty addition to the brick manor house with its moat and brick bridge. This dovecot had 750 'L'-shaped pigeon holes in the walls. Not all are as pretty as the one at Haslingfield but some are definitely quaint; for instance the one at Martin's Farm at Elsworth is rectangular and is built on a brick plinth and has a timber frame and boarded walls. It has a beautiful thatched saddle-back roof. The ground floor was used as a granary, the grain being kept in bins, with the pigeon loft in the roof. This could be approached up a ladder to a trapdoor in the ceiling and would have contained about 400 nest boxes. There is an example of an external loft built into the end wall of a barn at Dry Drayton with only 44 pigeon holes. Many Victorian farm buildings have pigeon holes in their gables which demonstrate that pigeon breeding continued on a small scale for domestic use and contributed meat for the farmer's family.

So the pigeon houses were made in whatever building material was available with walls of brick, clunch block, stone, or timber framed with lathe and plaster, or wattle and daub, and with thatch or peg tiled roofs. There was an alighting platform on the roof and the birds could enter through the lantern and then pass through a small trap door into the main hall.

Potted Pigeons

4 pigeons
1 level teaspoon mixed herbs
1/4 teaspoon nutmeg
salt and pepper
8 oz/225 g butter

Pack the pigeons into a casserole surrounded by the butter and sprinkle over the seasoning. Put on the lid and make sure it is very tight fitting; this can be done by making a flour and water strip of paste to put round the edge of the lid.

Bake in a cool oven at 300°F (150°C) Gas Mark 2 for at least 3 hours. Remove the pigeons and drain in a colander. Leave the butter in the casserole to solidify. Butter a terrine and take all the meat off the pigeon bones and put into it. Take the solid butter off the top of the casserole and melt it in a pan; pour it over the pigeons. Let it get quite cold and then turn out and serve. If you want to keep it for more than a week then cover the top of the pigeons with clarified butter. The pigeon bones can be returned to the juices in the casserole and made into soup.

Dovecot, Haslingfield

MEAT

> ### *This is meat for a Pope*
> ### *To boyle Ducks after French Fashion.*
>
> *Take and lard them and put them upon a Spit, and half roast them, then draw them and put them into a Pipkin, and put a quart of Clarret wine into it, and Chesnuts and a pint of great Oysters, taking the Beards from them, and three Onyons minced very small, some Mace and a little beaten Ginger, a little Time stript, a Crust of a French Roule grated put into it to thicken it, and so dish it upon sops. This may be divercified, if there be strong Broth there need not be so much Wine put in, and if there be no Oysters or Chesnuts you may put in Hartichock bottoms, Turneps, Coll flowers, Bacon in thin slices, Sweet Bread etc.*

"I sende owte my hawke this day to kill your parteridge for super on Monday", wrote one gentleman to his friend. The trained hawk was in great demand to supply the larder. All the Stuart Kings were fond of hawking, but it gradually ceased to be so popular later in the century owing to the great improvement in firearms. The hawk was a very dependable and untiring hunter, and the author of a treatise on hawking in 1619 says: "I have killed for the most part of a moneth together, with an intermewed goshawke (that is a hawk which moulted in captivity) eight, nine or ten partridges in a day".

Pigeons were no doubt a prey of the hawk too and they appear in all the old recipe books. They were good potted and this method was useful as they could be kept for a while and did not have to be eaten at once. There is a recipe in *The Country Housewife* written in the early eighteenth century, by Richard Bradley, Professor of Botany at Cambridge, for potting pigeons: "Season your pigeons with savoury spice, put them in a pot, cover them with butter and bake them; then take them out and drain them; when they are cold cover them with clarified butter". If you do not want to keep them you need not bother with the clarifying but have them cold with salad for a light summer lunch. Or the cooked meat can be made into a pâté with butter and brandy.

Mrs Beeton has 11 recipes for pigeons which were an inexpensive form of meat. A rather unusual way she suggests is to fry and casserole them and then add a sauce made with two dozen stoned olives which gives an interesting piquancy. They can be eaten with raisins, or prunes, or served with a morello cherry sauce.

Because they flew free they were at their best and plumpest in the early winter and did not have to be fattened for table like hens. There is a lovely description of how one lady fattened her hens: "To make them prodigiously fat in about twelve days My Lady Fanshaw gives them strong ale. They will be very drunk and sleep; then eat again. Let a candle stand all night in the coop, and then they will eat much all night".

Cooked Chicken in Cream of Curry Sauce

1¹/₂ lb/675 g cold cooked chicken
2 oz/50 g onion
1 tablespoon of oil
1 dessertspoon curry powder
1 tablespoon tomato paste
2 oz/50 g dried apricots, soaked
¹/₂ pint/275 ml mayonnaise
Large wine glass of red wine
Squeeze of lemon
Salt and pepper

Dice the chicken

Cook the onion in the oil gently, do not let it get brown. Add tomato paste, apricots chopped up if necessary, curry powder, wine and seasoning and let it simmer for a few minutes. Cool and then add the lemon juice and when cold fold in the mayonnaise. Pour over the chicken and stir gently till all the pieces are covered. Serve with a green salad, new or jacket potatoes, or fresh rolls.

Lady Fanshaw

To make good Sausages

Take the lean of a Legge of Pork, and four pound of Beef suet, or rather butter, shred them together very small, then season it with three quarters of an ounce of Pepper, and half an ounce of Cloves and Mace mixed together, as the Pepper is, a handful of Sage when it is chopt small, and as much Salt as you think will make them tast well of it, mingle all these with the meat, then break in ten Eggs, all but two or three of the whites, then temper it all well with your hands, and fill it into Hoggs gutts, which you must have ready for them, you must tye the ends of them like Puddings, and when you eat them you must boyle them on a soft fire, a hot will crack the skins and the goodness boile out of them.

Salads have always been eaten in England and salad stuffs grow well in the English climate. In the *Haven of Health* Cogan says: "Lettuce is much used in salets in the summer tyme, with vinegar, oyle and sugar and salt and is formed to procure appetite for meate, and to temper the heate of the stomach and liver".

Adam and Eve English delftware charger

Ham Galatine

3 cups of chopped cooked ham
3 hard boiled eggs
2 heaped tablespoons of chopped parsley
3/4 pint/425 ml ham stock
Freshly grated black pepper
1 packet powdered gelatine

Boil the eggs for 10 minutes and then plunge into cold water for a few minutes before taking off the shells and chop roughly.

Mince the cooked ham and mix with the eggs. Finely chop the parsley. Melt the gelatine and warm the stock; stir in the gelatine and pepper.

Sprinkle the parsley on the bottom of a loaf tin and pour on a little stock; put in the refrigerator to set. When set pack in the ham and egg mixture and pour over the rest of the stock and leave to set. To unmould put the tin in very hot water for a second and then unmould onto a serving dish. Decorate round the base with radishes or tomatoes and cucumber.

The range of salad herbs eaten was very wide, and Gerarde quotes over 30 in general use, some of which we recognize but do not use; "Chives, leeks, cresses, dandelion, endive, lettuce, spinache, dock, sorrel, purslane, borage, water pimpernel, bugloss, garden burnet and rosemary" and many more. Some of these like dock and sorrel would have to be picked when really young in the Spring, but this must have been the time when people were craving for variety in their diet after the long winter months.

In Stuart times John Evelyn wrote the standard treatise on the subject, *Acetarie*, a discourse on salads, and he says:

a salade is a Particular Composition of certain crude and fresh Herbs, such as usually are, or may be eaten with some Acetuous Juice, Oyle, salt etc to give them a grateful gust and vehicle. In the composure of a Salet, every plant should come in to bear its part, without being overpowered by some herb of a stronger taste, so as to endanger the native sapan and virtue of the rest; but fall into their places like the notes in music, in which there should be nothing harsh or grating; and the admitting some Discords (to distinguish and illustrate the rest) stricking in the more sprightly and sometimes gentler Notes, reconcile all dissonancies and melt them into an agreeable compotion.

So John Evelyn set down nearly 300 years ago these rules for making a good salad and they still hold good today and cannot really be improved upon. For the dressing he held that an artful mixture of mustard, oil and vinegar with or without the addition of hard boiled yolks of new-laid eggs, carefully rubbed into the dressing, "was all sufficient". He was most particular about the salad bowl, and thought it should not be of metal, silver or pewter but of "porcelaine or of the Holland Delftware".

MEAT

To make beefe like red Dear to be eaten cold

Take a buttock of beef, cut it the long waies with the grain, beat it well with a rowling pin, then broyl it upon the coals, a little after it is cold, draw it through with Lard, then lay in some white wine vinegar, pepper, salt, cloves, Mace and bay leaves, then let it lye three or four days, then bake it in Rye past, and when it is cold fill it up with butter, after a fortnight it will be eaten.

The rich pastures that lie at the end of the Cheddar Gorge provide excellent grazing for cattle and so the best cheddar cheese is made here. One early writer says that "the whole village of Cheddar were cow-keepers". Camden in his *Britannia* says that the Romans taught the British how to make cheese. Writing in 1586 he says: "West of Wells, just under the Mendippe Hills lies Cheddar, famous for its excellent and prodigious cheses made there some of which require more than a man's strength to put them on the table, and of a delicate taste, equalling if not excelling that of Parmesan".

Market Place, Wells

Cold Spiced Beef

2^1/$_2$ lb/1.1 kg skirt of beef
Either ^{1}/$_2$ tin of anchovies or 8 pickled walnuts
Cup of red wine
Bouquet garni
Salt and pepper

Buy 2 pieces of skirt of beef, trim off any fat. Lay one piece flat and place the anchovies or walnuts over it; place the other piece of beef on top and fold over into a Swiss Roll shape and tie several times with string; then tie string round it lengthwise.

Put into a casserole just big enough to take it, add wine, bouquet garni, salt and pepper and enough water to cover it and either let it boil very gently or put it in the oven for 3^1/$_2$ hours. Or it can be cooked in a slow cooker crock pot on high for ^{1}/$_2$ hour (using boiling water) and then on low for the rest of the time: 7 hours.

When done lift the beef out and let it drain and if possible press it flat by putting a chopping board on top and weights on top of that till it is quite cold. Untie strings carefully. Glaze and decorate if wished.

Remaining liquid will make into excellent soup.

Certainly by the seventeenth century they were much sought after and Lord Conway in 1635 wrote to Lord Poulet reminding him of a promised cheese, and Lord Poulet answered that these cheeses were held in such esteem at Court and by the nobility that they "are long bespoke before they are made". A few years later Sir Philip Percivalle asked his cousin to "bestow what surplus there may be from rents in the purchase of an old cheese called Cheddar". Daniel Defoe describes a monstrous cheese made for Lord Waymouth which, when it was scooped out, was big enough to hold a girl of 13. Queen Victoria was presented with probably the biggest Cheddar cheese ever made, it weighed 11 hundredweight, had a circumference of 9 feet, 4 inches and was 20 inches in depth.

The cheeses are made all through the summer months, from May onwards and through until the Autumn. The actual making is done over a period of 3 days and then they are stored on shelves. They have to be turned every day for 1 week and then turned twice a week for at least 3 months; there are farms in Somerset still making cheese in the traditional way, but the vast majority of Cheddar type cheese is made in factories as far apart as Sweden and Canada.

A small cheese is known as a Truckle and weighs between 7 and 10 pounds and this will ripen more quickly than a big cheese. The best time to buy a Truckle is in the Autumn. Of course, Cheddar cheese goes so well with Somerset cider, or Somerset apples.

Factory-made Cheddar is good for cooking and the more mature it is the more flavour or bite it has. There is an old recipe which is almost like a fondue which is very good.

Cut ^{1}/$_2$ lb cheddar into thin slices, put it in a pan. Add three tablespoons milk and one gill of cream, the yolks of three eggs and the whites of two, salt and pepper. Whip it till it boils and it is done.

This is good on squares of toast, or french bread.

MEAT

To Roast a Fillet of Veale

Take a Fillet of Beef which is the tendrest part of the beast, and lieth only in the inward Part of the Surloyne next to the Chyne, cut it as big as you can, then broach it on a broach not too big, and be careful you broach it not thorow the best of the meat, roast it leasurely and bast it with sweet Butter. Set a Dish under it to save the Gravy while the Beef is roasting, prepare the Sauce for it, chop good store of Parsley with a few sweet herbs shred small, and the yelks of three or four Egs, and mince among them the pill of an Orange, and a little onyon, then boyl this mixture, putting into it sweet butter, Vinegar, and gravy, a spoonfull of strong broth, when it is well boyled, put it into your beef, and serve it very warm, sometimes a little gross pepper or Ginger into your sauce, or a pill of an orange or Lemon.

John Speedy, the historian, gives a lovely description of Cheshire in the early seventeenth century; "meadows imbrodered with divers sweet smelling flowers, and the pastures makes the kines' udders to strout to the paile, from whom and wherein the best cheese in all Europe is made".

The soil of Cheshire contains rich deposits of salt and this affects the cheese so that it is slow to ripen but very long lasting. It is useful because it keeps so well and will last for weeks when cut without deteriorating. Samuel Pepys was very pleased when given a Cheshire cheese as a present, and Sir Kenelm Digby writing about the same time refers to it as a "quick, fat, rich, well-tasted cheese to serve melted upon a piece of toast". It is recorded that 300 tons of Cheshire cheese was ordered for the troops in Scotland during the Civil War and this must have been an easy and nourishing way of feeding an army.

Gloucester, west bridge and gate

58

Tournedos Béarnaise

4 1 inch thick slices of beef tenderloin
4 slices of bread
Butter for frying
2 egg yolks
2 tablespoons double cream
1 tablespoon tarragon vinegar
3 oz/75 g butter
1 teaspoon chopped tarragon
1/2 teaspoon chopped parsley
1/2 teaspoon chopped chives
Salt and pepper

Trim the bread to the same size as the beef slices, melt butter and fry them until they are golden brown. Fry the beef slices on each side until brown but leaving them rare in the middle; put them on the croutons. Serve with the following sauce.

In a bowl put yolks, cream, vinegar, salt and pepper, and fit the bowl over a pan of simmering water. Whisk until it begins to thicken then bit by bit add the butter stirring all the time. When melted and the sauce has become fairly thick add the herbs and serve.

Even until the end of the last century some farmers in Cheshire were paying their rents in cheese and also making sufficient for their own consumption to last a year. It is made in 3 colours, red, white and blue; the red has a vegetable juice added and takes a little longer to mature.

Double Gloucester was made in large sizes, up to 50 pounds in weight, and so needed at least 6 months in which to mature. It was made throughout the Vale of Gloucester, which is the low lying land around Berkeley and Thornbury which has a high rainfall. When ready it used to be sent down the Thames in barges from Lechlade to London.

The rinds were prepared in a curious way; in the cheese room the floor was prepared "by rubbing it with bean tops, potatoe halm, or other green succulent herbage, until it appears of a wet black colour". This was done in order to encourage "the blue coat to rise". Here the cheeses were turned twice a week, and the floor prepared afresh once a fortnight. By this method the rinds became "tough almost as leather", and therefore the cheese kept well and was free from cracks and protected from mites.

In some counties in England the soil is too light and sandy to make good pastureland and so any cheese made there is inferior. Suffolk is one such, and Pepys noted in his diary that the servants grumbled because his wife had given them Suffolk cheese. This prejudice continued to the days of Pope, whose country mouse entertained his courtly guest with,

Cheese such as men in Suffolk make,
But wished it Stilton for his sake.

To boyle a Capon larded with Lemons

Take a fair Capon and Truss him, boyl him by himselfe in faire water, with a little small Oat-meale, then take Mutton Broth, and halfe a pint of white Wine, a bundell of Herbs, whole Mace, season it with Vargels, put Marrow, Dates, season it with Sugar, then take preserved Lemons and cut them like Lard, and with a larding pin, lard it in, then put the Capon in a deep Dish, thicken your broth with Almonds, and powre it on the Capon.

I had rather live
With cheese and garlic in a windmill, far,
Than feed on cates, and have him talk to me
In any summerhouse in Christendom.

So Hotspur in Shakespeare exclaims and so today the simple meal of good bread and good cheese is still much appreciated.

Stilton is probably the most famous of all the English cheeses and a good ripe Stilton excels most other cheeses. Its origin is rather obscure but it is said to have first been made at Quenby Hall in Leicestershire and it was then known as Lady Beaumont's cheese. Lady Beaumont had a housekeeper called Mrs Ashby who married a farmer at Dalby and she handed down the recipe to her daughter who married a man called Paulet; she made the cheese and it was sold by her kinsman who kept the Bell Inn at Stilton. This Inn was a coaching Inn on the Great North Road and passengers disembarked for meals or to stay the night, and so the popularity and fame of Stilton cheese spread and it was taken and sold in London.

Summer and early Autumn are the best months for making cheese when the milk is naturally richest, later the grass wanes. Cheeses take months to ripen and the Stilton is in season or at its best from November to April. The cheeses were turned every other day in order that the curd should retain an even consistency, and every single day would be brushed in order to keep them clear of mites. The slow process of maturing goes on and takes about 6 months before the cheese is in perfect condition; then it will look a little brown at the rind and pale yellow and creamy inside. If it is cut too soon then it will be still hard, white and chalky, and the taste will be rather acid.

Stilton cheese is sometimes mentioned in literature; Jane Austin refers to it in "Emma" when Mr Elton describes to Harriet a party he had been to and had been given very good Stilton. Mary Lamb liked Stilton and there is a letter from Charles thanking Thomas Allsop for sending them a cheese, "the best I ever tasted – the delicatest, rainbow-hued, melting piece I ever flavoured".

Chicken with Orange and Tarragon

4 chicken quarters
1 large onion
1 oz/25 g butter
2 tablespoons oil
6 oz/175 g tin of orange juice
1 chicken stock cube
1/4 pint/150 ml water
3 pieces of fresh tarragon, chopped,
or 1 tablespoon of dried tarragon
1 tablespoon of cornflour
5 oz/150 g carton of sour cream

Trim the chicken pieces of all fat and skin. Melt butter and oil in a casserole and brown the chicken. Remove and keep on one side. Slice onion and cook in the casserole for about 5 minutes but do not let it get too brown, add orange juice, stock cube, and water and stir to melt stock cube, add tarragon and bring to the boil. Add chicken and cover. Put in the oven to bake at 350°F (180°C) Gas Mark 4 for an hour. Mix cornflour with 2 tablespoons of water. Take casserole out of the oven and remove the chicken pieces onto a serving dish. Stir cornflour into casserole so that it thickens, or bring to the boil again if necessary, stir well and take off the heat before adding the soured cream. Pour over the chicken pieces and serve.

Pewter mugs

Pottery wine flask used by travelling horsemen

To hash a Shoulder of Mutton

Take a Shoulder of Mutton and slice it very thin till you have almost nothing but the Bone, then put to the meat some Clarret wine, a great Onyon, some Gravy of Mutton, six Anchoves, a handfull of Capers, the tops of a little Tyme, Mince them very well together, then take nine or tenne Eggs, the juice of one or two Lemons to make it tart, and make leere of them then put the meat all in a frying pan over the fire till it be very hot, then put in the leere of Eggs and soak altogether over the fire till it be very thick, then boyle your bone, and put it on the top of your meat being Dished, Garnish your Dish with Lemons, serve it up.

Dorset Blue Vinny is one of the rarer and more romantic of the English cheeses and has to be nurtured rather carefully for it can only be made from the milk of cows grazing on the pasturelands around Sherborne. The roots of the grass get from the soil infinitesimal quantities of various mineral salts which make all the difference to the texture and flavour of the grass in the first place and of the milk and its cheese later. This is why Blue Vinny has always been a rare cheese. It can only be made in a small area during the summer months. It is a white cheese with royal blue threads running through it, and the blue colour is a mould. Old farmers used to say that a set of old harness, or leather that has not been used for years and which had a thick white mould upon it should be kept somewhere about if the cheese was to grow the bright blue threads.

Cambridgeshire cheese is a single cream cheese, soft and light, made in a roll about 4 inches in diameter, and can be bought by the yard. There used to be a Cambridge cheese made at Cottenham and called Double Cottenham; this is a cheese that is no longer available for during the war the U.S. Airforce took over the farms as part of an Air Base and scrubbed out the dairies with disinfectant and so destroyed the mould. A little farther north in Leicestershire there is good cheese, orange in colour and rather creamy and crumbly. The orange colour was originally made by putting a little carrot juice into the cheese and this makes it distinctive; it is pleasant and goes well with watercress.

Farther north again there is Dunlop. This was made first by Barbara Gilmour in the reign of Charles II. She had learnt cheese-making in Ireland, but had moved to Scotland at the time of religious troubles and settled in Ayrshire. She married and taught her family how to make cheese and so cheese-making became part of the way of life all around in the neighbouring farms. It has continued ever since. Dunlop is a creamy, mild version of Cheddar, with not so much bite, and is very good with Scottish oatcakes.

Lamb Chops with Apricot Sauce

6 lamb chops or escalopes of lamb fillet
4 oz/125 g dried apricots (soaked overnight)
1 oz/25 g dripping
1 level tablespoon curry powder
1 clove garlic
Juice of 1 lemon
1 oz/25 g sugar
2 sliced onions
3 tablespoons vinegar
salt and pepper

Cook the soaked apricots and sieve. Melt the dripping and fry the onions until cooked. Add all other ingredients and simmer gently for a few minutes. Pour over the raw lamb and leave to marinate overnight.

Lift out the meat and grill it for 4 minutes each side. Heat the sauce and pour over the lamb.

A farmer in Yorkshire recently, in 1985, found a ceramic pot buried in his cowshed, and in the pot were 1,500 gold and silver coins, a few dating back to the sixteenth century, the oldest being 1560. But there were also Spanish coins thought to have been brought over to England by Queen Henrietta Maria after her visit to the Spanish Netherlands to raise money for the Royalist cause. In the pot were also 2 receipts for 12 stone of cheese sold to the Royalist army and signed for by the Assistant Provider General and dated January 1643. So it seems the farmer supplied cheese for the troops and buried the proceeds in his cowshed but did not live to unearth them after the Civil War.

Royalist payment

To make a stumpe Pye

Take a Leg of Mutton, one pound and a halfe of the best Suet, mince both small together, then season it with a quarter of a pound of Sugar, and a small quantity of Salt and a little cloves and mace, then take a good handful of parsly, half as much Time and mince them very small, and mingle them with the rest, then take six new laid Eggs and break them into the meat and work it well together, and put it into the past, then upon the Top put Raisins, Currants and Dates a good quantity, cover and bake it, when it is baked, and when it is very hot, put into it a quarter of a pint of white wine Vinegar, and straw Sugar upon it, and so serve it.

At the beginning of the century the tableware of most households would have been simple and basic; dinner plates were mostly squares of sycamore wood hollowed out in the middle and a meat plate would be oval in shape and with a hollowed out well for gravy. Drinking vessels might have been of horn or mazers which were bowls of wood, often maple, and these could be banded with silver at the top so as to make them deeper. More exotic and curious cups were made out of polished coconut shells brought home from abroad by sailors and these would be given a rim of silver and mounted onto a silver stem with a flat foot and four bands of silver to hold it together.

Spoons were mostly of wood and sometimes were elaborately carved and given as love tokens to sweethearts. Pewter was also used for spoons. Spoons were an indispensable item of personal equipment as the host did not expect to supply them and so guests brought their own. Even as late as the 1660s Pepys took his own table silver with him when he dined with the Lord Mayor. A spoon was a common christening present and the saying "to be born with a silver spoon in his mouth" was probably first applied to those lucky infants whose godparents could afford to give them a silver spoon.

Leather wine bottles

Stuffed Shoulder of Lamb

1 shoulder of lamb (or leg if feeling extravagant)
1 onion
2 oz/50 g raisins
1 orange
3 oz/75 g brown breadcrumbs
1 egg yolk
1 teacup chopped parsley
Salt and pepper

Ask your butcher to take out the bone so that you can stuff the meat in the hollow left.

Thinly slice the onion and cook it gently in a little oil until soft. Grate the rind off the orange and squeeze out the juice. Mix all the ingredients together and stuff into the meat cavity. With a carpet needle and thin string make 3 ties to hold the meat together, or tie it up, or skewer together with cocktail sticks.

Melt a little fat in a roasting tin and put in the joint. Cook in a hot oven 425°F (220°C) Gas Mark 7 for 10 minutes and then turn the oven down to 350°F (180°C) Gas Mark 4 for 1 hour or more if the joint is a big one.

Forks did not appear until Tom Coryate brought back the two-pronged fork from Italy. The Victoria and Albert Museum in London have a silver fork with the London hallmark for 1632 and the 2 crests on the handle are those of Manners and Montague of Boughton, so it must have been the property of John Manners, later 8th Earl of Rutland, who in 1628 married Frances, daughter of Edward, Lord Montague of Boughton.

Pewter was used for spoons, plates, dishes, tankards and mugs; often it was very plain but sometimes with a pattern worked round the rim of the plate, or with a coat of arms worked in wriggle work on the rim or in the centre. Leather was used for holding liquids; it was coated with tar to make it waterproof and it was used for making bottles, jars, jugs, and the really large jugs for ale called black jacks.

Carving knives are still today sharp pointed at the top but other table knives are blunt and rounded. According to tradition Cardinal Richelieu was so disgusted by the Chancellor Seguier picking his teeth with his knife while at table that he ordered his Steward to round the end of every table knife in his household. Richelieu had tremendous influence on social manners as well as in national policy.

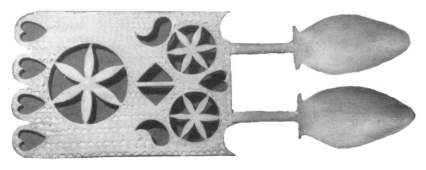

Lovespoons

A Turkish Dish

Take fat Beef or Mutton cut in thin slices, wash it well, put it into a pot that hath a close cover, then put into it a good quantity of clean pick'd rice, skim it very well, then put into it a quantity of whole pepper, two or three whole onyons, let all this boyl very well then take out the onyon and dish it in Sippets, the thicker it is, the better.

The glass industry in England improved and stabilized during the early part of the seventeenth century when the manufacturers changed the fuel they used from charcoal to coal. Whole forests had been cut down for charcoal burning. Glass bottles became more common, but the sale of wine in bottles was still prohibited. Wine was imported in casks and the purchasers took along their own bottles to the vintner to be filled. The early bottles had to be stoppered with wedge shaped pieces of wood or cork tied down with pack thread to the neck rim, or "string rim" of the bottles, with the ends protruding for easy removal. These bottles served simply as carafes for short-term rather than long-term storage. Simple corkscrews were in use by the end of the century but it was not until 1795 that Samuel Hurshell took out the first patent for a corkscrew design. This was a significant factor in the development of the wine bottle. An airtight seal could only be achieved with a drive in cork pushed fully into the bottle neck which could only be withdrawn clearly by a corkscrew. Wine could then be kept in good condition for long periods.

Early wine bottles

Turkish Lamb Kebab

1¹/₂ lb/700 g boned leg of lamb
1 onion
1 tablespoon dried rosemary leaves
1 teaspoon dried thyme
Juice of half a lemon
2 tablespoons olive oil
6 oz/150 g button mushrooms
salt and freshly ground black pepper

Cut lamb into cubes discarding all fat and very thinly slice the onion. Combine the olive oil, lemon juice, herbs, onion and salt and pepper. Add the lamb and leave to marinate for 3 hours, then brush the mushrooms with a little of the marinade. Divide into 4 portions and thread onto 4 kebab skewers leaving a small gap between the pieces. Heat grill and then put the skewers underneath and cook for 6 or 7 minutes turning frequently until the meat is brown on all sides.

Serve on a bed of rice, or inside toasted pitta bread, with a salad on the side.

Glass used for drinking glasses was all of the Venetian type and style known as "facon de Venise", or soda glass. It is rather thin and often has a bubbly appearance. This had been imported from Venice, but by 1635 was being made in England in large quantities and selling at half the price of the Venetian glass. The light Venetian style which had dominated the glass trade was suddenly revolutionized between 1675 and 1676 when a new glass "metal", or material was invented by George Ravenscroft at the Savoy Glasshouse in London. Though it was sold as "flint" glass, the traditional name for English glass, its new component was lead. This gave it a heavy, rich glossiness in contrast to the thin bubble-like hardness of the "facon de Venise" soda glass.

The elaborately wrought shapes of the light soda glass were impracticable for the slower-setting flint glass. A heavier simpler form evolved and this became the baluster glass of the eighteeth century. This was well proportioned with a deep bowl balanced on a singly or multi-knobbed stem often in the form of a baluster, and standing on a firm solid foot.

Earthenware Claret jug

To make a Calves Chaldron Pye

Take a Calves Chaldron, half boyl it, and cool it, when it is cold mince it as small as grated bread, with a half pound of Marrow, season it with Salt, beaten Cloves, Mace, Nutmegge, a little Onyon, and some of the outmost rynd of a Lemond minced very small, and wring in the juice of half a Lemond, and then mix all together, then make a peece of puff Past, and lay a leaf therof in a silver Dish of the bigness to contain the meat, then put in your meat, and cover it with another leaf of the same Past, and bake it, and when it is baked take it out, and open it, and put in the juice of two or three Oranges, stir it well together, then cover it again and serve. Be sure none of your Orange kernells be amongst your Pye-meat.

There are many references in *The Queen's Closet Opened* to the use of silver basins, pots, plates, dishes and so on during cooking; a thing we would not dream of doing nowadays, but then we have non-stick saucepans and attractive oven-to-table ware. The recipe above uses a silver dish on which to make a pie with pastry underneath and on top. This sort of pie would be difficult to transfer from one dish to another and so it was cooked on a silver dish and taken straight to the table looking respectable.

Silverware had its ups and downs during the seventeenth century. Under the Stuarts all sizeable households had their silver and we have an inventory of the silver belonging to the Fairfaxes at Walton taken in 1624. Thomas Stagges, who was in charge of the plate, records a list of "the plate which stood upon the cupboard in your chamber". Amongst them were:

A silver bason and ewer, a silver chaffin dish, a dozin silver plaites, a silver pott with two eares, a silver candle stick, six silver saucers, one great spown and two lesse spownes for preserving with, five spownes which were kept for the children, two large porringers of silver. Two lesse silver porringers, a litle silver boat, a sugar box of silver, a litle childes possnet of silver with three feet.

It is not difficult to picture the Fairfaxe family at dinner using the silver from the cupboard; the 5 children with their 5 spoons of silver and the youngest using the possnet bowl with 3 feet.

There is also an entry for "a silver morter and pestell" weighing 43 oz 22 dwt which must have been quite large and substantial, but we do not know if it lived in the cupboard or the kitchen, or perhaps in the Stillroom to be used when making herbal remedies and medicines.

Steak and Smoked Oyster Pie

1 lb/450 g steak
$^1/_4$ lb/125 g kidney
1 tin smoked oysters
Oil for frying
1 packet frozen flaky pastry
Salt and pepper

Cut the meat into dice about an inch square, and the kidney half that size. Coat with flour and fry in hot oil until brown. Put in a casserole and just cover with water and cook for 1 $^1/_2$ hours.

Put the meat into a pie dish and reduce or thicken the gravy if necessary and pour over the meat. Stir in the oysters and allow to get cold.

Roll out the pastry and make a top for the pie dish, decorating it with a pattern and making one or two slits for the steam to escape. Brush with milk or a mixture of egg yolk and water. Put in a hot oven 450°F (230°C) Gas Mark 8 for 10 minutes and then turn the oven down to 375°F (190°C) Gas Mark 5 for a further 15 minutes.

It is sad that so much of this sort of family silver went into the melting pot for the Parliamentary or Royalist cause when they were urgently raising money to pay for armaments, clothes and food for their troops. During the period of strife great quantities of gold and silver were melted down, and even when peace came with the commonwealth period of 1649–60 the spirit of Puritanism was so severely utilitarian that only comparatively plain pieces were made. The total quantity made during this time was quite small, but with the Restoration the wealthy began to buy silver again, and there were many new people who were wealthy. Decoration increased and production soared.

Silver dish

To make an Out-landish Dish

Take the Liver of a Hogg, and cut it in small peices about the bignes of a span, then take Ani-seed, or Fennell-seed, Pepper and Salt, and season them therwithall, and lay every peice severally round in the cale of the Hogg, and so roast them on a Bird-spit.

For nearly 700 years the keepers of the King's plate, or more exactly the guardians of its quality, have been the Worshipful Company of Goldsmiths in London. Under Edward the First in the year 1300 there was a statute that directed that:

No vessels of gold or silver should leave the maker's hands until they had been tested by the Wardens and stamped with the leopard's head.

There was a declaration that the marks were to be struck only on "good sterling silver". An Assay Office was at once set up and the practice of the assay came to be universally respected. The members of the Goldsmiths' Company were also respected and continued to increase in affluence as well as influence.

The obligation to mark silver with the maker's initials and a date letter originated in, or about, 1423, and at that time it was ordered that York, Newcastle, Lincoln, Norwich, Bristol, Salisbury and Coventry were to have "divers touches".

All went well for over 300 years until the Civil War when so much gold and silver was melted down, and then with the Restoration and the return of Charles II there was a sudden upsurge of demand. Not only did the households of the wealthy want silver but ordinary inns and taverns wanted silver tankards and drinking vessels. To meet this sort of demand the less scrupulous silversmiths resorted to the very simple expedient of melting down the coinage of the realm. This practice became so common that it assumed the proportions of a public scandal. In the end, on 25 March 1697 the government passed into law an Act under which all wrought silver had to be made from an alloy consisting of 11 oz 10 dwt of fine silver and 10 dwt of copper to the pound troy. This settled the whole matter and the shortage of silver coins came to an end.

The new standard silver was ordered to be marked with special punches, and for a time the use of the leopard's head and of the lion passant was suspended. The Higher Standard silver was marked with a figure of Britannia for the office, and with the lion's head erased as a guarantee of quality, and pieces marked like this are still called "Britannia" silver.

Pork Tenderloin with Mushrooms

2 lb/900 g pork tenderloin
1/2 teaspoon thyme
salt and pepper
3 oz/75 g fine white breadcrumbs
2 eggs, beaten
4 oz/100 g butter
8 oz/225 g mushrooms
1 tablespoon chopped parsley

Cut the tenderloin slantwise into 1/2 inch thick slices and rub each with salt and pepper. Mix the thyme with the breadcrumbs. Dip the pork slices into the beaten egg and then into the breadcrumbs pressing firmly. Melt half of the butter and fry the pork gently for about 3 minutes on each side; when they are golden brown remove and keep hot. Melt remaining butter and fry the mushrooms for 2 minutes then serve with the pork.

Pork cooked like this can also be served cold; in which case marinate the mushrooms, sliced, in a marinade of olive oil, vinegar, salt, pepper, mustard and tomato paste.

Silver porringer and lid

To make a Chickin Pye

Take four or five Chickins, cut them in peices, take two or three Sweet-breads parboyl'd and cut in peices as big as Wallnuts; take the Udder of Veale cut in thin slices or little slices of Bacon, the bottoms of Hartichoaks boyl'd, then make your Coffin proportionable to your meat, season your meat with Nutmeg, Mace and Salt, then some butter on the top of the Pye, put a little water into it as you put it into the Oven and let it bake an hour, then put in a leer of butter, Gravy of Mutton ,eight Lemons sliced; so serve it.

The diary of Samuel Pepys gives a wealth of detail about the life and customs of the times and it tells us that he was never above giving or receiving a consideration for a favour and the consideration often seems to have taken the form of a piece of silver. He was a promising young administrator of the Restoration and rose fast as an official in the Admiralty. There is a reference to a visit to the goldsmith Backwell to buy "£1OO worth of plate for my Lord to Secretary Nicholas", and we are told that when it came to be delivered it was accompanied by Pepys' "own piece of plate, being a state dish and cup in chased work for Mr Coventry, cost me above £19".

That was in 166O and 4 years later Pepys had reached a position which made it worthwhile for other people to solicit his favours; a Mr Falconer visited his wife and brought her a present of a silver state-cup and cover, value about £4, for the courtesy Pepys did him the other day. But the state-cup did not satisfy the Pepyses and so the next day they took it to Backwell's and changed it for a "fair tankard". Not long after Mr Gauden, who was a victualler to the navy, gave them a "rich present of two silver and gilt flaggons". Mrs Pepys was not in when they arrived but when she returned her husband showed them to her "to her great admiration and joy", and he adds "indeed (they) are so noble that I can hardly think they are yet mine".

Silver sconce

Turkey and Chestnut Pasty

6 oz/175 g chestnuts
1¹/₂ lb/675 g cooked turkey
2 tablespoons stuffing
3 tablespoons thick gravy
12 oz/350 g flour
3 oz/75 g lard
3 oz/75 g margarine

Cut the tops off the chestnuts and boil them for about 30 minutes; then skin them while still hot.

Dice the turkey and stuffing and mix with the chestnuts and turkey gravy.

Make up the pastry and roll out on a floured board and divide into 2 rectangles one bigger than the other. Put the turkey filling on the smaller of the two but not quite coming to the edges; dampen the edges and place the bigger piece on top and press down the edges and crimp upwards to seal. Decorate the top with any extra pieces and make one or two holes in the top for steam to escape. Brush over with egg or milk. Put in a greased meat tin and bake in a fairly hot oven at 400°F (200°C) Gas Mark 6 for about 25 minutes. Serve with more gravy made out of turkey stock.

Silver was also given on special occasions and Pepys writes that he travelled to Walthamstow with 6 spoons and a porringer of silver in his pocket to give to a god-child at its christening. Later there is an entry that he paid £10 14s for a silver christening bowl "for my wife to give to the parson's child, to which the other day she was god-mother".

Portrait of Samuel Pepys by Kneller

There are many more entries about presents from people who wanted favours, or orders; there were two large candlesticks and snuffers and a "slice" which was a tray, to put them on, from Mr Harris who was the sail-maker to the navy; a Captain Cocke honoured a long-standing promise of a present of 12 plates, and Mr Foundes gave a pair of candlesticks and half-a-dozen plates. It is the last entry about a present of silver which is the most notable; it reads:

"On 1st January 1669 – presented from Captain Beckfors, with a noble silver warming pan, which I am doubtful whether to take or no". A silver warming pan was, and is, a very rare piece indeed. Did Pepys accept it, and if not, why not?

To make a Steak Pye with a French Pudding in the Pye

Season your Steaks with Pepper and Nutmegs, and let it stand an hour in a Tray, then take a peece of the leanest of a Legg of Mutton, and mince it small with Suet and a few sweet herbs, tops of young Time, a branch of Penny-royall; two or three of red Sage, grated bread, Yelks of Eggs sweet Cream, Raisons of the Sun, work altogether like a Pudding, with your hands stiff, and roul them round like Balls, and put them into the Steaks in a deep Coffin, with a peece of sweet Butter, sprinkle a little Vergis on it and bake it, then cut it up and roul Sage leaves and fry them, and stick them upright in the walls, and serve your Pye without a Cover, with the juice of an Orange or Lemond.

Oliver Cromwell as Lord Protector had a Court as all the other countries in Europe had, and automatically assumed the rights of Kingship though he did not use them extensively. New honours were conferred; for instance, Charles Howard, one time captain of the protector's life guard and the grandson of a peer, was made a viscount. Also one of his cousins was made a baron. He adopted a much quieter and plainer life-style and this was reflected in the fashions of the time and not only in clothes but also in furniture and furnishings, and what little gold and silver ware that was made was noticeably plain and lacking decoration.

Cromwell's court consisted of many of the old nobility and it is reported that "The Marquis de Lede, Lord Ambassador of the King of Spain, had audience by His Highness in the Banqueting House in Whitehall, where were the greatest assembly of English nobility and gentry present that have been these years". Special entertainments were laid on at the Protectoral court for special occasions, and the most frequent of these was for the reception of foreign ambassadors. These receptions were splendid in their settings, but fairly plain and short compared with those of Charles I or Charles II. The Dutch envoy and his wife and daughter were entertained by Cromwell in April 1654. The Masters of Ceremonies went to fetch them in 2 coaches at about half past one and brought them to Whitehall where 12 trumpeters were ready and sounded their arrival.

Oliver Cromwell

Veal and Bacon Terrine

1 lb/450 g lean belly pork
1 lb/450 g lean veal
1/2 lb/225 g streaky bacon
teacup white wine
2 tablespoons brandy
2 or 3 cloves of garlic
1/2 teaspoon thyme
1/2 teaspoon marjoram
pinch of mace
salt and pepper
bay leaves

Mince all the meat coarsely except for about 3 strips of bacon. Crush the garlic and add to the meat, add the herbs, salt and freshly ground black pepper. Stir and add the wine and brandy, stir well and leave to soak for at least 2 hours.

Arrange bay leaves and strips of bacon on the bottom of the terrine, pack in the mince and put on the lid. Place the terrine in a meat dish of cold water (half-way up the sides) and cook for about 2 hours in a moderate oven at 325°F (170°C) Gas Mark 3.

Carefully pour off fat and juices before unmolding; it will have shrunk away from the sides a little while cooking. Decorate with parsley round the base.

They were received by his Highness with the "greatest demonstration of amity". After a little conversation they were shown into another room where a table was laid. Cromwell sat on one side of it alone; two Lords and the Dutch envoy sat at the upper end and the Lord President Lawrence and others further down. There was in the same room another table for other lords of the Council. At the table of the Lady Protectress dined Lady Newport, Lady Lambert, the Dutch envoy's wife and daughter and Cromwell's daughter.

Music was played all the while as they were at dinner. Afterwards they retired to another room with the ladies, and they had music and wine and a psalm was sung. Later they moved into a gallery next to the river and walked with his Highness for about half an hour before taking their leave. They were conducted back to their house in the same manner as they were brought, and it sounds from the report that the Dutch were very pleased with this reception.

Cromwell's youngest daughter married Robert Rich, the grandson of the Earl of Warwick and restrictions seem to have been eased for the occasion. The wedding feast was at Whitehall, and there were 48 violins and 50 trumpets and "much mirth with frolics, besides mixed dancing (a thing heretofore accounted profane) till five o'clock the following morning".

To make a Batalia Pye

Take four tame Pigeons and Truss them to bake, and take four Ox Pallats well boyled and blaunched, and cut it in little peeces, take six Lamb-stones, and as many good sweet Breads of Veale cut in halfs and parboyld, and twenty Cockscombs boyld and blanched, and the bottoms of four Artichokes, and a Pint of Oysters parboyld and bearded, and the Marrow of three bones, so season all with Mace, Nutmeg and Salt, so put your meat in a Coffin of fine Past proportionable to your quantity of meat, put half a pound of Butter upon your meat, put a little water in the Pye, before it be set in the Oven, let it stand in the Oven an hour and a half, then take it out, pour out the Butter at the top of the Pye, and put it in a leer of Gravy, Butter, and Lemons, and serve it up.

At the beginning of the century the popularity of madrigals was waning but new secular songs and "catches" were being written, and the Court was the focus of patronage. The masques put on at Court needed composers and musicians as well as writers and designers. Religious music continued through the Commonwealth years and was allowed at Court by Oliver Cromwell; psalms were sung for visiting Ambassadors.

At Court and at large houses music was often played throughout meals by professional musicians, and there was much music-making by ordinary people. An educated man was expected to be able to play a lute, viol or other instrument, or hold a part in a madrigal or song. In homes, taverns or on board ship unaccompanied songs, often in 3 parts, were sung.

After the Restoration when the theatres opened again, music featured as part of many of the plays. Pepys went to see "The Virgin Martyr" and wrote:

That which did please me beyond anything in the whole world was the wind musique when the angel comes down, which is so sweet it ravished me, and indeed, in a word, did wrap up my soul so that it made me really sick that neither then, nor all the evening going home, and at home, I was able to think of anything, but remained all night transported, so that I could not believe that ever any musique hath then real command over the soul of a man as this did upon me; and makes me resolve to practise wind musique and make my wife do the like.

The Queen's Catholic Chapel

Veal and Ham Pie

4¹/₂ oz/140 g plain flour

3 oz/90 g butter

1 egg yolk

or

12 oz/375 g frozen puff pastry

1 egg yolk

1 lb/500 g stewing veal, diced

1 oz/25 g butter

2 onions

1 tablespoon flour

2 cups water

2 chicken-stock cubes

2 teaspoons mustard

1 tablespoon tomato paste

2 teaspoons mixed herbs

salt and pepper

4 oz/125 g ham, diced

2 tablespoons chopped parsley

Heat butter in a pan, add veal and brown; add chopped onions and sauté until tender; add flour, stir and let it cook for 2 minutes. Remove pan from heat and stir in water, add stock cubes, mustard, tomato paste, herbs, salt and pepper. Return to the heat and stir until sauce boils and thickens then cover and simmer for 50 minutes stirring occasionally. Take off the heat and add ham and parsley. When cold fill the pie. Rub butter into flour, add egg yolk and then water and mix to a dough; roll out on a floured board to fit an 8 or 10 inch pie plate, spread filling evenly. Roll out puff pastry and arrange over pie pressing edges together, trim and decorate, make a slit in the top of the pie and brush with egg yolk mixed with a little water. Bake at 450°F (230°C) Gas Mark 8 for 10 minutes then reduce heat and bake for a further 15 minutes until golden brown.

He was a competent musician and practised hard on viols, violin, lute, theorbo and flageolet and was duly proud of also composing. Many evenings in the Pepys household were spent with friends having a good supper with plenty to eat and drink, and then music making. Several times he mentions going to the Queen's Chapel: "I took my wife to St. James' and there carried her to the Queen's Chapel, and heard excellent musick". Another time: "To the Queen's Chapel, and there did hear the Italians sing, and indeed their musick did appear most admirable to me beyond anything of ours: I was never so well satisfied in my life with it".

PUDDINGS

To make a green Pudding

Take a penny loaf of stale Bread, Grate it, put to halfe a pound of Sugar, grated Nutmeg, as much Salt as will season it, three quarters of a pound of Beef suet shred very small, then take sweet Herbs, the most of them Marrigolds, eight Spinages, shred the Herbs very small, mix all well together, then take two Eggs and work them together with your hand, and make them into round Balls, and when the water boyles put them in, serve them, Rosewater, Sugar, and Butter for Sauce.

Beehive ovens for baking bread can still be seen in the backyards of houses in villages in Turkey, and in remote parts of Greece and Spain. They are brick-lined and so hold the heat a long time and are most effective and economical. They were used in England until the advent of gas and electric cookers and were sometimes built alongside the kitchen chimney or else in a special bake-house.

Baking day, usually once a week, was very much part of the rhythm of the household. A small fire of kindling would be started on the floor of the oven and gradually built up with sticks and then logs. After about 1½ hours the oven would be really hot with a nice red glowing fire in the centre. The door would be opened and the fire raked all over the floor and the door shut again for about 10 minutes; this would distribute the heat evenly over the floor. Then the door would be opened and the red hot ashes raked out and the floor of the oven mopped over quickly with a wet cloth or mop. The door was shut again for it to dry for a few minutes and then the bread put in and left to bake for 1½ hours. When taken out it would be crisp on the outside and sound hollow when tapped.

Cottage hearth – note the brick lined oven

Hot Pineapple Pudding

Large tin of pineapple cubes
2 oz/50 g flour
2 oz/50 g butter
2 oz/50 g sugar
2 eggs

Drain the pineapple juice through a sieve into a basin and measure out just short of 1/2 pint/225 ml.

Cream the butter and sugar until light and then beat in the egg yolks. Gradually add the flour and finally the pineapple juice; it will probably curdle but it does not matter. Beat the egg whites till they are stiff and fold them into the mixture.

Pour it into a buttered dish and stand the dish in a meat-tin of cold water. Bake in a moderate oven 350°F (180°C) Gas Mark 4 for about 40 minutes. It will rise to make a light soufflé top with pineapple sauce underneath.

Ten minutes before serving put the pineapple cubes in a dish in the oven to heat through and serve them with the pudding.

After the bread in would go pies and pastries, followed by cakes and biscuits.

In the summer and autumn fruit in bottles would go into the oven to cook and sterilize just as Kilner jars did before the days of freezers. As the heat died down the oven could be used for drying off things such as apples, or feathers, and finally in would go the kindling ready for next week's bake day.

It was obviously very convenient and economic of time and effort to use the oven once a week and so have food cooked and ready for several days' consumption. It needed good forward planning and careful timing on the part of the cook and her helpers to have things prepared and ready to go in the oven one after another. There would be time to make pastry while the bread baked, and time to make biscuits and little cakes, with help from the daughters perhaps, before taking out the pastry pies and pasties, and so on to the custards or bottled fruit. Households tended to be large and children numerous and so an established routine helped their smooth running.

To make an Almond Pudding

Take your Almonds when they are blanched, and beat them as many as will serve for your Dish, then put to it foure or five yelks of Eggs, Rose-water, Nutmeg, Cloves and Mace, a little Sugar, and a little Salt, and Marrow cut into it, and so set it into the Oven, but your Oven must not be hotter then for Bisket bread, and when it is half baked, take the white of an Egge, Rose-water and fine Sugar well beaten together and very thick and do it over with a feather, and set it in again, then stick it over with Almons, and so send it up.

Kitchens then, as now, needed many utensils to make cooking easier. Natural things like twigs or rushes were bound together to make whisks but other equipment had to be specially constructed.

The cook would need an oven peel which was a long handled flat spade made out of wood which she could use for fishing loaves out of the hot oven. Also a bake stone or griddle which she would get really hot and then use for cooking little flat cakes or scones on, cooking first one side and then turning them over to cook the other side. Fire irons were most necessary and large 2 pronged forks were used to stir the fire or rearrange peat or faggots.

Copper was used to make conical ale mullers with long handles so that they could be set in the hot peat or embers to heat the spiced ale. Copper was also used for great mixing bowls; these were rather more than half-spheres so that the ingredients of a great cake could be well beaten. A large bowl was needed when you took a "peck of flower", 3 pounds of butter, a quart of cream and 16 eggs.

Cupboards for storing food were made to hang up on the wall out of the reach of dogs and mice. They had open fret-work or spindles for ventilation. In the Gatehouse of a large house there might be a dole cupboard; food would be put in it regularly so that the poor could collect it.

Hanging dole cupboard

Figgy Pudding

4 oz/125 g suet
8 oz/225 g flour
1/2 pint/275 ml milk
6 oz/175 g dried figs
2 oz/50 g dried apricots
1 oz/25 g dried apples
4 oz/125 g prunes
2 oz/50 g dates
3 oz/75 g raisins and sultanas
1 tablespoon honey
1 wineglass brandy
1/4 teaspoon ginger
1/4 teaspoon cinnamon

The day before making the pudding put the apricots, prunes and apples to soak in water and put the raisins and sultanas to soak in the brandy.

Put a large saucepan one-third full of water on to boil. Take stones out of the dates and prunes; butter a large pudding basin. Mix the suet and flour then add the milk gradually to make a fairly stiff dough; roll out and line the pudding basin leaving sufficient aside to make a top. Melt the honey and stir in the ginger and cinnamon, add the brandy mixture. Pack the fruit into the basin and pour the honey mixture over it. Put the suet-crust lid on the basin, then cover with foil and tie down tightly leaving a long end of string to make it easy to lift out of the saucepan later. Put the basin in the boiling water and cook for 2 hours watching that it does not boil dry. Turn out onto a dish and serve.

During the summer in the country the midday meal would be taken out to the workers in the fields. Cider or light ale was taken out in small barrels called costrels, some of which are still in use on remote farms. Horn mugs were used in the fields and were almost unbreakable. Pasties, bread and cheese and apples formed these simple meals.

Outdoor equipment was needed to ensure a supply of food for the larder; traps, snares and hingles for catching larks. Bait such as hemp seed was laid across a field and then a length of twine laid on top of it. From the twine were short lengths of hair from horses, manes and tails each ending in a noose made with a running knot; this would catch the feet of the feeding birds. They must have taken infinite patience, and probably small fingers, to construct.

Baker's peel

To make poor Knights

Cut two penny loaves in round slices dip them in half a pint of Cream or fair water, then lay them abroad in a dish and beat three Egs and grated Nutmegs and sugar, beat them with the Cream, then melt some butter in a frying pan, and wet the side of the toasts and lay them in on the wet side, then pour in the rest upon them, and so fry them, serve them in with Rosewater, sugar and butter.

The idea of boiling a pudding in a buttered cloth originated in a Cambridge college in 1617 and revolutionized cooking for now a sweet pudding could be boiled alongside the main course of a meal in one large cauldron. This method must have been an enormous help in smaller households of limited means for boiled suet puddings were filling, nourishing, hot and cheap. They were, no doubt, welcomed by undergraduates in Cambridge too. A recipe in *The Queen's Closet Opened* suggests this method.

Before this hot puddings were mostly of batter, fried as pancakes or fritters, or else as a coating for fruit. Apples or pears would be threaded on to a thin bird spit and put to roast, and the cook would dribble a thick batter over them so that it formed a crisp coating. Or dried fruit like apricots and raisins with walnuts or almonds were threaded on a string and wound round the spit and then the batter poured over them to cook.

Baking pastry

Bread, Butter and Banana Pudding

4 slices of white bread

2 oz/50 g butter

1 banana

3 oz/75 g sultanas

2 eggs

1 egg yolk

1/2 pint/275 ml milk

1 oz/25 g sugar

1 or 2 tablespoons rum

Grated nutmeg

Cut the crusts off the slices of bread and butter them; cut into 4 triangles. Butter a pie dish and put in a layer of buttered bread, sprinkle on half the sultanas and half the banana; repeat and then end with a layer of bread butter side up.

Beat the eggs, sugar, milk together and then add the rum. Pour over the bread, grate on the nutmeg and leave to stand for one hour.

Bake in a moderate oven at 350°F (180°C) Gas Mark 4 for about 30 minutes by which time it should be well risen and golden brown.

The old book has a recipe for making Poor Knights; the Poor Knights were an order founded by Edward III in 1349 for military pensioners who lived in small apartments in Windsor Castle. Their name suggests that they had to live frugally and this pudding is a way of using up stale bread. It is on record that the present Prince of Wales shares this taste, and has been known to try his hand at cooking bread-and-butter pudding – with bananas added.

Pies and tarts were made when the oven was lit and filled with whatever fruit was available, or had been stored or preserved; apples and quinces were much used, or apples and lemon rind, or pill as it was called then. Pumpkin pie was eaten in the Autumn and the Pilgrim Fathers took some seed over to America and had it for their Thanksgiving dinner for their first harvest in the New World and it has been on the menu ever since. Mince pies were traditionally eaten at Christmas and the New Year but actually contained meat minced, or the old book suggest Neat's tongue and plenty of suet and currants.

Open tarts filled with preserves were made in many traditional designs like the lattice, or the crenellated where the edge was cut every inch and the alternate pieces turned in towards the centre. Taffety tarts had pastry tops which when cooked were taken out and brushed with melted butter and rosewater and strewn with sugar and popped back into the oven to glaze so that they would shine like taffeta.

To make a Pumpion Pye

Take about half a pound of Pumpion and slice it, a handfull of Tyme, a little Rosemary, Parsley, and sweet Marjorum slipped off the stalks, and chop them small, then take Cynamon, Nutmeg, Pepper and six Cloves, and beat them, take ten Eggs and beat them, then mix them, and beat them altogether, and put in as much Sugar as you think fit, then fry them like a froize, after it is fryed, let it stand till it be cold, then fill your Pye, take sliced Apples thinne round wayes, and lay a row of the Froize, and layer of Apples with Currants betwixt the layer while your Pye is fitted and put in a good deal of sweet Butter before you close it, when the Pye is baked, take six yelks of Eggs, some Whitewine or Vergis, and make a Caudle of this, but not too thick, cut up the Lid and put it in, stir them well together whilst the Eggs and Pumpions be not perceived, and so serve it up.

The very early cookery books have some nice little asides and directions for the cook and they also tell us a little more about the things they used in their kitchens and the sort of people who had to use them. One speaks of "leather aproned cooks" who seem a long way away from our white coated Chefs.

Before you set the liquor to boil cause a lusty servant, (his arms well washed) to mix the honey with the water labouring it with his hands at least an hour without intermission.

Put sweet thick cream into a dish and whip it with a bundle of white hard rushes (of such as they make whisks to brush cloaks) tied together, till it come very thick in about a good hour will serve in winter, in summer it will require an hour and a half.

Servants needed to be lusty and persevering.

Another way of beating cream was with a bundle of reeds "tyed together and rowle between your hands standing upright in your cream".

There are different sorts of boiling described; for instance when making a rice pudding with milk "make it stew or boil simpringly for an hour or more". But for oatmeal gruel "let it boil long, till it be almost boiled enough, then make it rise in a great ebullition, in great galloping waves, and skim off all the top that riseth".

For boiled parsnips you should:

grate them and add a little milk and simmer and when all the milk is imbibed add a little more and so on till it is a pulpe and well swelled. Eat them so without sugar or butter, for they will have a natural sweetness that is beyond sugar, and will be Unctuous, so as not to need Butter.

Creamy Lemon Pie

80 oz/224 g flour
2 oz/50 g lard
2 oz/50 g margarine
2 medium sized parsnips
2 lemons
1/4 pint/150 ml milk
1 teaspoon honey
1 tablespoon sugar
2 egg yolks

Peel the parsnips and thinly slice them leaving out any really hard core. Put in a pan with half the milk and gently cook; after 10 minutes add more milk if necessary and continue cooking until the parsnip is a soft pulp. Add sugar and honey and beat well, then add egg yolks and beat again. Grate the rind off the lemons and squeeze out the juice; add to the mixture. Make up the pastry and roll out on a floured board and with it line a greased flan tin. Pour in the lemon mixture and smooth flat; with remaining bits of pastry make strips, twist them and lay them in a lattice pattern across the top of the pie; brush with milk to make them shiny and bake the pie in a moderate oven at 400°F (200°C) Gas Mark 6 for about 20 minutes until nicely brown. Serve either hot or cold.

To boil eggs:

a certain and infallible method to boil new laid eggs to sup up, and yet that they have the white turned to milk is thus: break a very little hole at the bigger end of the shell, and put it into water while it boileth. Let it remain boiling whiles your Pulse beateth two hundred strokes. Then take it out immediately and you will find it of exact temper. Others put eggs into boiling water just as you take it from the fire and let them remain there till the water be so cooled that you may just put your hand and take out the egg.

There is also a recipe for boiling apples; first you peel them and then boil them very gently and so "boil your pippins until they be tender, that you may prick a rush through them". So many things such as reeds and rushes from the countryside came into the kitchen, but most important of all the cook had to be careful of her fire and is told "in the heating of milk be careful of smoaks".

Copper mixing bowl

Lambeth Delft drug pot. (Royal Institution of Cornwall)

Henrietta Maria after Van Dyck, c. 1632-5.

(Reproduced by courtesy of the National Portrait Gallery, London).

Court dress of silver tissue with Venetian lace collar and feather fan, 1660.

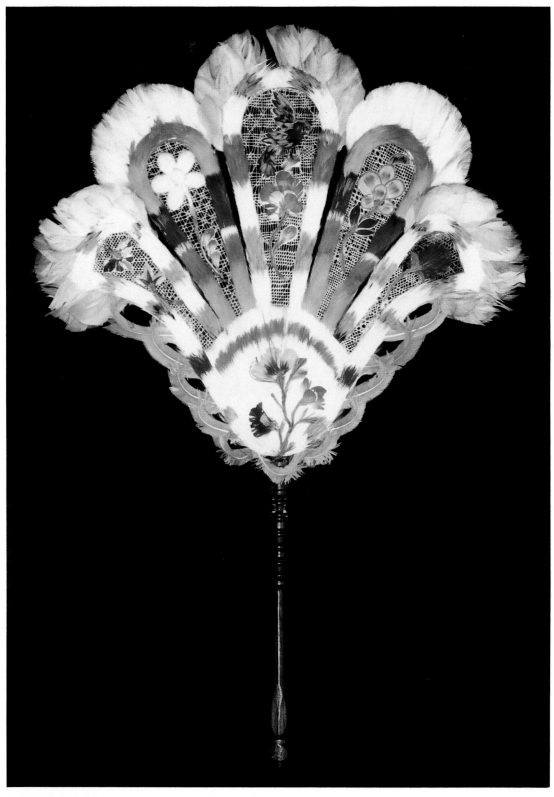

Fan c. 1625. The frames are covered with exotic feathers composed to look like flowers and birds, and are quite different on each side.

The Dining Room in St. Fagans Castle, Cardiff.

(Reproduced by kind permission of the Welsh Folk Museum).

'The Tea Party', attributed to Richard Collins.

Grace Cup 1616 (maker's mark: FB)

(Reproduced by kind permission of the Worshipful Company of Goldsmiths)

The Seymour Salt, silver gilt c. 1662.

(Reproduced by kind permission of the Worshipful Company of Goldsmiths)

Chinoiserie porringer and cover, London, 1680

(Reproduced by kind permission of the Worshipful Company of Goldsmiths)

The State Bedroom, Powys Castle, Powys, as decorated for Charles II with gilded rails to keep off the multitude.

(photo by Jeremy Whitaker, Reproduced by kind permission of The National Trust).

Blickling Hall, Norfolk, built 1619-29, showing the long east front and formal garden.

(Reproduced by kind permission of The National Trust and Alister Burg).

Dressing room tapestry at Houghton Hall showing James I, Charles I and their Queens.

(Reproduced by kind permission of The Marquis of Cholmondley).

Southwick in the County of Southampton the Seat of *Richard Norton Esq.*

Southwick, Hants showing gardens and woods. (Bodleian, Douce Prints a 24 plate 74)

The French Barley Cream.

Take a quart of Cream, and boyle in a Porrenger of French Barley, that hath been boyled in nine waters, put in some large Mace and a little Cynamon boyling it a quarter of an hour, then take two quarts of Almonds blanched, and beat it very small with Rose-water, or Orange water, aud some Sugar, and the Almonds being strained into the Liquor put it over the fire, stirring it till it be ready to boyl, then take it off the fire, stirring it till them be half cold then put to it two spoonfuls of Sack or white Wine, and when it is cold, serve it in, remembring to put in some salt.

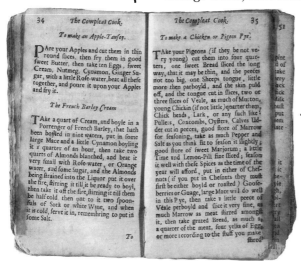

On several occasions in the original cookery book the cook is advised to add rosewater to her blanched almonds when she is going to pound them in a mortar to "keep them from oyling". Today we set almond cakes upon white rice paper and let them cook to a gentle brown but then they "set them on brown paper and they will look whiter". When making biscuits the cook must "then prick them with a pen made of wood, or if you have a comb that hath not been used, that will do them quickly, and is best to that purpose".

If making a jelly of Harts Horn :"You may try it with a spoon if it will jelly, you may know by the sticking to your Lips".

There are 1 or 2 directions on how to serve food usually on a silver dish or in a silver basin or porringer. There is one recipe that tells the cook to dish up a turkey and then "they are wont to lay it on a napkin folded square, and lay it cornerwise". Elsewhere there is an account of a young couple who have moved into a grander house and had their dining room hung with green serge and gilded leather going off "buying of a tablecloth and a dozen napkins of diaper, the first that ever I bought in my life".

There were various uses in the kitchen for feathers: "Then if you perceive any fat to remain and swim upon it clense it away with a feather". When the Marchpan is made and is cold and hard then "ice him with rosewater and sugar and so spread him with a wing feather". Pastry seems to have been made fairly tough and hard for there were no patty tins and the pastry was shaped into "coffins" to hold a filling. If these coffins were to be baked empty and filled later with fruit or a preserve then bran was put into them to keep them in shape while in the oven "and when they are hardened, take them out, and with a Wing brush out the bran".

Feathers were used elsewhere in the house and so were always kept when poultry and birds were plucked for the table. They would be sorted and dried out if necessary – the softer feathers were used in vast quantities for making mattresses. The beds were hard and so a really thick feather mattress must have been most

Praline Creme

Almond rock
2 oz/50 g almonds
3 heaped tablespoons sugar
2 tablespoons water
3 eggs
1 tablespoon sugar
small carton double cream
1 pkt (1/4 oz) gelatine

Blanch almonds in boiling water and take off the skins. Bake almonds or gently grill them until they are well browned. Heat sugar and water and boil until mid-brown. Add almonds and pour on to a well buttered plate. Leave to get cold. Then crush between greaseproof paper with a rolling pin.

Beat egg yolks and sugar in a basin over hot water until thickened; let it get cold.

Melt gelatine in 1/4 pint water. Let it get cold. Beat cream until thick. Beat egg whites until stiff. Fold egg yolks, gelatine, almond rock and cream together, then fold in egg whites gently with a metal spoon. Pour into a glass bowl and serve with finger biscuits.

State bed slept in by Charles I while staying in Brecon

welcome especially in the winter. Pillows were also stuffed with feathers, and they also had "woolsacks" which were cushions stuffed tightly with wool.

After more than 4 centuries a wool sack, a large square bag of wool without back or arms and covered with cloth is still the usual seat of the Lord Chancellor in the House of Lords. This signified the position of the Lord Chancellor as the highest judicial officer and he was sitting on the wealth of the nation, namely wool.

To make Clouted Cream

Take four quarts of Milk, one of Cream, six spoonfuls of Rose-water, put these together in a great Earthen Milk Pan, set it upon a fire of Charcoale well kindled, you must be sure the fire be not too hot, then let it stand a day and a night, and when you go to take it off, loose the edge of your Cream round about with a Knife, then take your board, and lay the edges that is left beside the board, cut into many peeces and them into the Dish first, and scrape some fine Sugar upon them, then take your board and take off your Cream as clean from the Milk as you can, and lay it upon your Dish, and if your Dish be little there will be some left, the which you may put into what fashion you please, and scrape good store of Sugar upon it.

Clowtyd crayme and nawe crayme put together, is eaten more for a sensuall appetyte than for any good nouryshement.

Boorde.

In one present day family clotted cream is certainly a "sensuall", or texture experience for they put it thickly upon digestive biscuits, top it with chocolate spread and call it Devonshire Lust.

Clotted cream is a speciality of Devon and Cornwall where there is a high rainfall and rich pasture for the cows. There is also local peat for the farmhouse fire which burns slowly with the gentle heat ideal for cream making. The evening milk is put into broad earthenware pans and the next morning is set over a slow fire where it will remain the whole day, never boiling but just heating gently. The steady heat of the earthenware pan is excellent for cream-making and will cool down equally slowly too. The pan is taken off the fire and put on the stone-flagged floor of the dairy overnight. The next day the cream has risen to the wide top of the pan and is thick and crusty.

Scallop shells were used to lift the clotted cream off the milk underneath. These shell fish are to be found around the Devon coast and the flat naturally grooved shells make excellent cream lifters. The milk underneath may be fed to calves or piglets.

In the recipe here it is called Clouted Cream and a clout is a thick patch, usually associated with leather and of course, the cream does wrinkle up into thick leathery folds. It was eaten then as a dessert just with sugar strewn on it. We like it with fruit or on new white bread or scones with strawberry jam. Certainly its colour and texture are its main attractions.

Raspberry and Hazelnut Pavlova

3 oz/75 g hazelnuts
5 egg whites
pinch of salt
9 oz/250 g castor sugar
4 oz/100 g plain flour
2 tablespoons sherry
1/2 pint/300 ml double cream
1 tablespoon icing sugar
12 oz/350 g raspberries

Prepare a loose-bottomed cake tin (9 in) by lining it with non-stick baking paper. Mince hazelnuts. Whisk the egg whites and salt until the mixture forms stiff peaks, lightly whisk in the castor sugar and then with a fork fold in the flour and hazelnuts. Pour into the cake tin and bake in a moderate oven 350°F (180°C) Gas Mark 4 for about 40 minutes and test with a skewer. Leave it to cool for 15 minutes and then turn out on to a wire rack, when cold put in the fridge to chill.

Shortly before serving cut it in half horizontally with a sharp knife which has been dipped in hot water. Sprinkle the cut sides with sherry. Whip the cream and icing sugar until thick. Reserve a few raspberries for decoration, and fold the remaining ones into the cream; put half this mixture onto the bottom layer of pavlova and place the second layer on top, cover with remaining cream mixture and decorate with raspberries. Chill until it is served.

It is not always available and so we use more double cream to make quick and delicious desserts – serve it with bananas, whitecurrants and brown sugar, or whip it with brown sugar and pour it over little seedless green grapes. At Eton and at King's College, Cambridge, they enjoy a traditional delicacy made of double cream whipped to a soft peak consistency, a couple of tablespoonfuls of icing sugar folded in and then 1 1/2 pounds of strawberries cut fairly small folded into that and chilled. It emerges from the fridge a luscious pink "Strawbery Mess".

Ravenscroft glass platter

To make Jelly of Harts Horn

Take six ounces of Harts Horn, three ounces of Ivory both finely carped boyle it in two quarts of water in a Pipkin close covered, and when it is three parts wasted, you may try it with a Spoon if it will jelly, you may know by the sticking to your Lips, then strain it through a jelly Bag; Season it with Rose-water, juice of Lemons and double refined Sugar, each according to your Tast, then boyle altogether two or three wames, so put in the Glass and keep for your use.

Spit with baskets for sauce making

Strawberry Water Ice

2 lb/900 g strawberries
1/2 lb/225 g sugar
1/4 pint/150 ml water
Juice of 1 lemon

Boil the water and sugar for 5 minutes and let it get cold. Sieve the strawberries through a nylon sieve and add to the syrup. Add the juice of the lemon. Pour into ice trays and cover with foil, or into ice-lolly moulds, and refrigerate for about 2 hours till frozen, or freeze in freezer.

If ice-cream is wanted then whip 1/4 pint/150 ml of double cream and add to the water ice mixture. Freeze and after about 1 hour take out and stir well to break down any ice crystals and freeze again.

At night come to Abingdon, where had been a fair of custard;
and met many people and scholars going home.

This was in June 1668 in a region of rich pastureland, but a whole fair of custard seems excessive. Many of the puddings of the time were custards or creams of various sorts, such as syllabubs made with cream and cider or sack, or junket made with cream, curdled with rennet and flavoured with rosewater. Blancmange was made with rice, eggs, cream, sugar and almonds and so was much more interesting and richer than ours today.

Jellies were made in moulds and were served at banquets, but they must have been laborious to make when the setting agent was boiled calf's foot, or very finely shaved hartshorn (antler). They would have been flavoured and coloured by fruit such as raspberries and strawberries. Flummery was an easier kind of jelly to make; oats or wheat were soaked, boiled and strained and the liquid would then set. It would be flavoured with orange, lemon or perhaps wine and later with brandy. In poorer households the soaked grain would be included in the dish making it porridgy.

Charles I had an Italian chef who made a water ice, the first in England, which was a sweetened fruit juice frozen.

A Tansy took its name from the plant which is rather bitter tasting and was used medicinally. The pudding continued without the original ingredient of tansy and was a mixture of cream, butter, eggs, sugar and fruit, usually apple with cloves or nutmeg. It was cooked and served hot with the top browned with a salamander.

Cheesecakes were served in London eating houses and would have been curd cheese in a plain pastry case and maybe a little flavouring. Eating houses were very numerous in large cities and whole meals could be bought and taken home, or bakers would cook a person's joint for a very small sum. When coal was used for cooking rather than wood, then a more sophisticated spit would be used. At each end there would be an upright pillar on top of which was a small iron basket just big enough to hold a few glowing coals taken from the fire. Over this the cook could cook in a saucepan or skillet and make a sauce or custard

To make a great Curd Loaf

Take the Curds of three quarts of new milk clean wheyed, and rub into them a little of the finest flour you can get, then take half a race of Ginger, and slice it very thin, and put it into your Curds with a little Salt, then take half a pint of good Ale Yeast and put to it, then take ten Eggs but three of the Whites, let there be so much flour as will make it into a reasonable stiff Past, then put it into an indifferent hot cloath, and lay it before the fire to rice while your Oven is heating, then make it up into a Loaf, and when it is baked, cut up the top of the Loaf, and put in a pound and a half of melted Butter, and a good deal of Sugar in it.

If people lived out of London then shopping could pose quite a problem, and husbands and sons were often asked to buy things when they were there, or else to carry letters to shop keepers or pay bills. Margaret Paston asked her son in London to let her know the price of pepper, cloves, mace, ginger, cinnamon, almonds, rice, saffron and "raysonys of Corons". These things may have been cheaper in London than in Norwich, and she was a careful, thrifty housewife. Small but expensive things like spices could easily be carried in the pockets or saddlebags of someone riding, so she asked her son "send me word what price a pound. If it be better cheap in London than it is here, I shall send you money to buy such stuff as I will have". Frequently she asked for sugar loaves, "I pray you that you will vouchsafe to send me another sugar loaf for my old is done".

Treacle was also asked for but this was used medicinally. She wrote to her husband: "I have sent my uncle Berney the pot of treacle that you did buy for him. Also I pray you heartily that you will send me a pot with treacle in haste for I have been right evil at ease, and your daughter both, since you rode hence, and one of the tallest young men in the parish lieth sick and has a great myrr". A myrr was a heavy cold. Sir John sent home 3 pots of treacle of Genoa. There is in the old book a recipe for Dr Butler's Cordial Water which was to be given "to one sick of the Plague, it driveth all venome from the heart". In it is used half a pound of Venice treacle with Pimpernel, Cardous, Angelica, Scordium, Scabious and Dragon distilled in Rosewater. It was to be taken blood-warm.

Stores had to be bought for the winter and one letter refers to a Lenten supply of dried fish which would be used for breakfast: "As for herring, I have bought an horse-load for four shillings and six pence. I can get no eels yet". Also the Bailiff wrote offering to buy for her:

Mistress, it were good to remember your stuff of herring now this fishing time I have got me a friend in Lowestoft to help to buy me seven or eight barrel, and (they) shall not cost me above six shillings and eight pence a barrel. You shall do more now (Autumn) with forty shillings, than you shall at Christmas with five markes, or sixty-six shillings and eight pence.

Another lady received a letter from her London cloth-mercer recommending some sarcenet which was a very soft silk.

Madame, the sarcenet is very fine, I think it most profitable and most worshipful for

Hot Chocolate Pudding

5 oz/150 g flour
2 teaspoons baking powder
1/2 teaspoon salt
6 oz/150 g sugar
3 tablespoons cocoa
1/4 pint/150 ml milk
2 oz/50 g butter
1 teaspoon vanilla

Topping
4 oz/125 g sugar
3 tablespoons cocoa
3/4 pint/425 ml boiling water

Melt butter. Sift together the dry ingredients and then add the butter, milk and vanilla. Mix the batter until smooth. Grease an ovenproof dish and pour in the batter. Mix together the additional sugar and cocoa and sprinkle over the batter. Then pour over the boiling water. Do not stir, leave it on the top. Bake in an oven at 350°F (180°C) Gas Mark 4 for about 40–45 minutes.

The batter rises up into a cake with the topping sinking into a sauce underneath.

you and shall (last) you your life and your child's life after you, whereas the harlatry of forty or forty-four pence a yard would not endure two seasons with you. Therefore a little more cost, me thinketh most wisdom to take of the best.

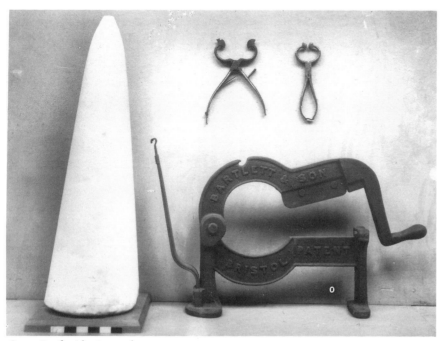

Sugar Loaf with vice and cutters

To make a Quaking Pudding

Take a Pint and somewhat more of thick Creame, ten Eggs, put the whites of three, beat them very well with two spoonful of Rose-water, mingle with your Creame three spoonful of fine flower, mingle it so well, that there be no lumps in it, put it altogether, and season it according to your Tast, Butter a Cloth very well, and let it be thick that it may not run out, and let it boyle for halfe an hour as fast as you can, then take it up and make Sauce with Butter, Rose-water and Sugar, and serve it up.

You may stick some blanched Almonds upon it if you please.

The Queen brought new fashions into England not only in styles but also in fabrics and colours. She liked softer, more flowing clothes than had been the fashion in previous decades, and accessories such as lace collars and cuffs became soft and draped or gathered. Stiff ruffs, wires and hoops were out and skirts reverted to easy, graceful lines; wasp waists disappeared as the Queen was almost always pregnant. As a girl she had been rather thin and always remained small in stature, but she blossomed into a real beauty as the happiness of her marriage increased. She was careful in choosing the colours she wore, dressing to her skin tone of dark brunette; we see her in her portraits wearing oyster white with scarlet ribbons, or carnation pink, or glowing amber. She made fashionable all shades of russet and coral, and soft smokey blues. These simpler dresses needed really good fabrics, good quality silks which often came from France, satins and taffetas, damasks and velvets, camlets and velours. During this century more furs were imported and were worn for warmth – cloaks were lined with fur and the Queen had a little cape lined with ermine.

Mica fan

Steamed Orange Pudding

1 large tablespoon of golden syrup
Rind and juice of 2 oranges
4 oz/100 g butter
4 oz/100 g sugar
4 oz/100 g flour
2 oz/50 g fine breadcrumbs
2 eggs

Butter a large pudding basin. Melt the golden syrup and add orange rind and juice and pour into prepared basin. Beat butter and sugar until light and gradually add beaten egg. Add flour and breadcrumbs. Put this mixture into the basin with the orange sauce and cover with a double layer of kitchen foil and tie down tightly with string, leaving a long end to make it easier to lift. Lower the basin into a large saucepan of boiling water, sufficient to come well up the basin. Put the lid on the saucepan tightly, but check occasionally that it does not boil dry. Boil for 1½ hours and then turn out on to a dish big enough to take the pudding and the surrounding sauce.

Hairstyles too became simpler with no more false hair and elaborate coiffures but the hair twisted into a knot worn high on the back of the head and with little ringlets falling softly round the face.

Clothes were no longer sewn with jewels and jewellery was no longer worn in abundance, but what was worn was simple and magnificent. The Queen liked pearls and had a string that were very big and perfectly matched, and had a pair of large drop earrings which appear in several portraits. When she went into exile much of her jewellery was sold to raise money for arms and troops for her husband's cause and at her death there was nothing very remarkable in her jewel chest except her great cross of diamonds and her pearls.

Henrietta Maria was not so very extravagant about clothes, compared with Elizabeth I who had over 3,000 dresses in her wardrobe when she died, and if she liked a dress she would continue to wear it for a couple of years. Where she was wildly extravagant was in the costumes created for her masques; these were extremely opulent, very expensive and vast amounts of materials were used. She never seemed to think about the cost and often the bills were not paid for years.

An excellent Sillabub

Fill your Sillabub pot with Syder (for that is the best for a Sillabub) and good store of Sugar and a little Nutmeg, stir it well together, put in as much thick Cream by two or three Spoonful at a time, as hard as you can, as though you milk it in, then stir it together exceeding softly once about, and let it stand two hours at least ere it is eaten, for the staning makes the Curd.

One or two old inventories survive and tell us that a widow left 3 gowns, 5 petticoat skirts, a safeguard (apron), a cloak, 2 hats, 3 waistcoats, "wearing linen and other necessities". A man's outfit was a hat, a doublet, a jerkin, 2 pairs of breeches, 1 of leather and 1 of wool, 2 shirts, 4 bands and 2 pairs of shoes.

The diary of Samuel Pepys tells us a good deal about his clothes; he says he obeys "Osborn's rule for a gentleman". Francis Osborn wrote in *Advice to a Son*; "Wear your clothes neat, exceeding rather than coming short of others of like fortune; a charge borne out by acceptance where ever you come. Therefore spare all other ways rather than prove defective in this". Early in his career Pepys had to be thrifty but took care to look well dressed. On 29 April 1660 he writes: "This day I put on first my fine cloth suit made of a cloak that had like to have been dirtied a year ago, the very day I put it on". So a stained cloak was made up into a suit. Three months later he writes "This morning came home my fine Camlet cloak with gold buttons, and a silk suit which cost me much money, and I pray God to make me able to pay for it". Camlet was a material made of a mixture of silk and wool and very expensive; a few years later he had a suit made of Camlet which cost £24.

Hats seem to have mattered a great deal to the gentlemen of the time and Pepys bought one costing 35 shillings. Stubbs wrote:

As the fashions be rare and strange, so are the things where of their hats be made, diverse also: for some are of silk, some are of velvet, some are of taffety, some of sarcenet, some of wool and which is more curious, some of a certain kind of fine hair, these they call beaver hats, of twenty, thirty or forty shillings price, fetched from beyond the sea.

Beaver hats were made of beaver fur or some imitation of it.

Lemon Syllabub

4 oz/125 g castor sugar
2 lemons
Small glass of brandy
1/2 pint/275 ml double cream
pinch of cinnamon

Day 1 Grate the rind of the lemons and squeeze out the juice and put both into a bowl with the glass of brandy.

Day 2 Put castor sugar and a pinch of cinnamon into the bowl and stir. Whip the double cream until thick, and still whipping very slowly add the lemon mixture. Put in the fridge.

Day 3 Serve with finger biscuits.

Lady Katherine Paston was most concerned that her son who was up at Cambridge should have a Beaver hat and writes in a letter "as for a beaver hat, if you could fitt your selfe with a spetiall good on I would be very content".

Memorial to Lady Paston in Oxmead Church

Lady Paston sent her son "Sweet Will" a new suit of satin, silk stockings, garters, shoe strings and a silver girdle, and tells him to have great care to wear his clothes clean and neat, without spots and dirtiness. The following year she sent him a damask suit and urged him to be sparing in the wearing of it. She also sent a cake, a cheese, a few puddings, a turkey pasty, a pot of quinces and some "marmelate"; so mothers, student sons and tuck-boxes have not changed much over the centuries.

To make Pyramidis Cream

Take a quart of water, aud six ounces of Harts horn, and put it into a Bottle with Gum-dragon, and Gum-arabick, of each as much as a small Nut, put all this into the Bottle, which must be so big as will hold a pint more; for if it be full it will break, stop it very close with a Cork, and tye a Cloth over it, put the Bottle into a Pot of Beef when it is boyling, and let it boile three hours, then take as much Cream as there is Jelly, and half a pound of Almonds well beaten with Rose-water, so that you cannot discern what they be, mingle the Cream and the Almonds together, then strain it, and do so two or three times to get all you can out of the Almonds, then put jelly when it is cold into a silver Bason, and the Cream to it, sweeten it as you like, put in two or three Grains of Musk and Amber-Greece, set it over the fire, stirring it continually and skimming it, till it be seething hot, but let it not boyle, then put it into an old fashion drinking Glass, and let it stand till it is cold, and when you will use it, hold your Glass in a warm hand, and loosen it with a Knife, and whelm it into a Dish, and have in readiness a Pine Apple blown and stick it all over, and serve it in with Cream, or without as you please.

During the long and peaceful reign of Elizabeth I large country houses were built which reflected the settled peace of the country after the period of the Wars of the Roses. They no longer needed to be fortified and their gardens could spread out around them. The Italian Renaissance influence can be felt in the arrangement of these gardens. They were laid out in geometric designs usually round an axis which related to the main facade of the house so that order and colour was laid out immediately beyond and below the windows.

The knot garden evolved and this consisted of rectangular arrangements of beds, often 4, and each of the 4 compartments were filled by an intricate design of little hedges of closely clipped evergreen box. The spaces in the middle of these designs were filled in with coloured gravels. In the late Spring the box would produce its tiny heavily scented flowers and the whole knot would be alive with bees and butterflies. Of course, these gardens took a good deal of work to keep them immaculately prim and tidy, but they gave all the year round colour and harmony to the garden.

Melon and Raspberry Sorbet

1 large Melon
1 lb/450 g raspberries
1/2 lb/225 g loganberries or redcurrants
1 lemon
4 oz/125 g sugar
1/4 pint/150 ml water

Melt the sugar in the water and bring to the boil, let it cool and add the lemon juice.

Purée the raspberries and loganberries and add to the syrup. Put in a plastic bowl and freeze until nearly set — about 40–50 minutes. Take it out and beat it well with a wooden spoon to break down any ice particles; put it back in the freezer.

Take the top off the melon and scoop out all the pips; put it in a dish and decorate by sticking flower heads such as marigolds or dog daisies round the outside of the melon. Fill with the sorbet and serve. Scoop out some of the melon flesh with each serving of sorbet.

There was one at Hampton Court and Cardinal Archbishop Wolsey walked there on fine evenings with his Chaplain and said his office. This was later built over. There is another one there now and the box-edged beds are filled with the silver green of lavender and the brighter silver leaves of southernwood.

Bacon was rude about them and wrote: "they be but toys; you may see as good sights many times in tarts". But they are very attractive and have a fascination. They could be constructed in a small town garden and would be very interesting to create. There is one that was laid out in 1975 at Barnsley House, near Cirencester, from Stephen Blake's design of 1664 in his book *Complete Gardener's Practice*. It has great charm and elegance and forms one of a series of interesting features in this very beautiful garden.

Knot garden at Barnsley house

The Lord Conway his Lordships recipe for the making of Amber Puddings.

First take the guts of a young hog, and wash them very clean, and then take two pound of the best hogs fat, and a pound and a half of the best Jurden almonds, the which being blancht, take one half of them and beat them very small and the other half reserve whole unbeaten, then take a pound and a half of fine Sugar and four white loves, and grate the loves over the former composition, and mingle them well together in a bason, having so done, put to it half an ounce of Amber-greece, the which must be scrapt very smal over the said composition, take half a quarter of an ounce of levant musk and buise it in a marble morter, with a quarter of a pint of orange flower water, then mingle these all very well together, and having so done, fill the said guts therwith, this Receipt was given his Lordship by an Italian for a great rariety, and has been found to be by those Ladies of honour to whom his Lordship has imparted the said reception.

The knot garden was superseded by the "parterre" which was larger and grander and perhaps a little vulgar. The great practitioner of this style was Louis XIV's gardener, Andre Le Notre who created the gardens at Versailles, St. Cloud and Fontainebleau. They were, of course, on a vast scale and needed an army of gardeners.

Parterres were set out in geometric outlines hedged with clipped box or some other small shrub, but the designs inside each compartment now became more flowing and this could be done as they were on a much larger scale. Gardening books of the time illustrated designs that could be used. The patterns were set out in little hedges and the centres filled in with smaller shrubs or flowers. There were long grass or gravel walks between the beds, and sometimes statues or fountains as centre or corner points. The whole pattern could be seen to advantage from the windows of the house.

Formal knot garden

Glass Pudding

2 oz/50 g butter

8 oz/225 g crushed biscuits

2 tablespoons golden syrup

1 tablespoon cocoa

Melt the butter, add the syrup and then the cocoa and crushed biscuit and beat well. Grease a shortbread tin and put the mixture in, pressing well down.

2 oz/50 g butter

3 oz/75 g castor sugar

1 tablespoon cocoa

Beat butter till light and add in sugar and cocoa. Spread over the first layer.

3 oz/75 g sugar

4 tablespoons water

Boil together until golden and then quickly pour over the pudding but do not scrape out the pan too much or the sugar will crystallize and spoil the "glass" effect of the top. To serve cut into slices with a strong knife when cold and eat the same day or the top tends to go sticky.

This type of garden needed a flat site and this was not always easy to find in England and so this kind of design had to be adapted or made considerably smaller than its French counterpart. Two French gardeners produced designs for Hatfield House and Wilton House, but both gardens were replaced once they were out of fashion in the next century

The Dutch also favoured parterres and they provided much scope for a formal spring garden of bulbs. Bulbs became increasingly common at this time and the Dutch were producing more and more varieties. There was a great vogue for planting tulips as they were being bred in more colours and shapes and heights; in fact the development of tulips had become something of a mania and people were paying high prices for the latest or more exotic varieties. They were used widely as a decorative motif on porcelain or pottery, in needlework or in flower pictures at this time.

Bulbs were imported in very large numbers during the last quarter of the century and there are old bills in existance for "200 junquiles at six shillings a 100, 200 tulips at five shillings a 100; 100 Dutch crocus and 12 striped fillerayes".

In England the parterre gave way gradually to flower beds as we know them now and there was always less formality than in Holland and France. The English landscaped garden as advocated by Capability Brown in the next century really suited the English countryside and the English people much better

PUDDINGS

To make Cream with Snow

Take three pints of Creame and the whites of seven or eight Eggs and strain them together, and a little Rosewater, and as much Sugar as will sweeten it, then take a stick as big as a Childs arm, cleave one end of it a cross, and widen your peeces with your finger, beat your Cream with this stick or else with a bundle of Reeds tyed together, and rowle between your hand standing upright in your Cream, now as the Snow ariseth, take it up with a Spoon in a Cullender that the thin may run out, and when you have sufficient of this Snow; take the Cream that is left, and seeth it in a Skellet, and put thereto whole Cloves, sticks of Synamon a little Ginger bruised, and seeth it till it be thick, then strain it, and when it is cold put into your Dish, and lay your Snow upon it.

Herb gardens were cultivated in monasteries and the herbs used not only in cooking but also for making the medicines used in their hospitals. Many of them were very effective such as the use of our common Meadowsweet which chemists in the last century synthesized and called aspirin. Some of their leaves or roots were used for making dyes. Many were used for their scent and were dried and put into "sweet bags" which were kept amongst linen or clothes stored in chests, as we have seen at Hardwick. These "sweet bags" were often made of the most beautiful needlework and given away as presents.

Knitting in the garden, Wells Cathedral Close

Lemon Snow

1 lemon jelly

2 lemons

3 egg whites

Skin the rind off the lemons and put with 1/2 pint of water and bring to the boil. Pour through a sieve into a bowl, add the jelly and melt it. Add the juice of the lemons and let it get cold and nearly set. Whisk the egg whites. Put jelly and egg whites into a large bowl and whisk very hard (preferably in a cold room or draught) until it has trebled in volume and is nearly white in colour. Pour into a large glass bowl and put in the fridge to finish setting. Decorate with very thin slices of lemon and serve with small meringues and cream.

Herbs were included in posies as it was believed they would ward off the plague; certainly they would help to overcome the unpleasant smells encountered in many streets. Judges were presented with nosegays to have by them in Court which was perhaps necessary when dealing with so many unwashed prisoners. Fleabane was strewn on the floors of coaches for obvious reasons.

Often the herb garden would be set apart surrounded by a clipped yew hedge and laid out in a pattern. This could be squares or rectangles, or in a circle like a wheel with a different herb planted in between each spoke of box hedging. If there was a garden seat this would make a good place for a quiet conversation, or to do some needlework in the sun.

Herbs were not restricted to the herb garden, however, for when trees were planted as alleys, which were to make shady walks, then herbs were planted underfoot. In his essay, "Of Gardens" Bacon says that "those which perfume the air most delightfully, not passed by as the rest, but being trodden upon and being crushed are three; that is burnet, wild thyme and watermints". They can still be used to give us fragrance in this way, and there are several thymes which grow flat and sprawl and should be welcome on a patio or terrace. The wild thyme usually called Thyme Drucie by nurserymen will grow flat and spread into a 2-foot circle and has little pink to red flowers. There is also the lemon-scented Herbabarona, or Thymus minimus which has small woolly leaves and is a good ground hugger. A really showy variety is called Golden Carpet and has a rich yellow foliage that spreads well. All sun loving and good for walking on.

To boyle Cream with Codlings

Take a quart of Cream and boyle it with some Mace and Sugar, and take two yelks of Eggs, and beat them well with a spoonful of Rose-water and a grain of Amber greece, then put it into the Cream with a peece of sweet Butter as big as a Wallnut, and stir it together over the fire untill it be ready to boyle, then set it some time to coole, stirring it continually till it be cold, then take a quarter of a pound of Codlings strained, and put them into a silver Dish over a few coales till they be almost dry, and being cold, and the Cream also, poure the Cream upon them, and let them stand on a soft fire covered an hour, then serve them in.

This century was one where there was much experimentation in the cultivation of fruit trees and there was an increasing interest in importing them or growing them from seed collected in Europe; we know that one gentleman when travelling in France enjoyed an apple so much that he kept the seed and successfully grew it up into trees when he got home. There was also development in the skill of grafting trees.

Lambeth palace (Bodleian, Douce Prints a 24. plate 8)

Apricot Creme

2 oz/50 g dried apricots
1 tablespoon sugar
2 eggs
$^1/_2$ pint/275 ml milk
$^1/_2$ teaspoon vanilla essence
small carton double cream
2 oz/50 g dark chocolate

Soak the apricots in a little water overnight.

Cook apricots with sugar till soft; put them in the bottom of a soufflé dish. Whisk eggs, milk, vanilla and a little sugar (if liked) and pour gently into the soufflé dish and cover with foil tightly. Put the dish in a tin of boiling water and put in a medium oven 300°F (150°C) Gas Mark 2 until set firm.

When cold whip cream and pour on top. Grate the chocolate and sprinkle on the cream. Keep cold in the fridge

John Evelyn was a great observer and noted that in the fertile and well watered gardens at Beddington, near Croydon, the pomegranate bore fruit. Turner a century earlier says there were pomegranates "in my Lord's garden at Syon, but their fruit cometh never to perfection" so perhaps it was not in a position with sufficient sun. He also says that there were "divers fig trees in England in gardens, but nowhere else", so they did not grow wild. There are massive and very flourishing fig trees on the south wall of the Library of Lambeth Palace in London which were planted by Archbishop Pole during his Primacy, 1554–58, which prove they are very long lived. These are the white Marseilles variety that ripen well. In the garden at Montacute there is a long wall covered with fig trees, and these would have been eaten raw or preserved for winter use. There is nothing quite like a really ripe fig eaten straight off the tree, just slightly warm from the sun.

Turner also writes about what he calls an "abricok": "me think seeing that we have very few trees of this as yet it were better to call it an hasty peach tree, because it is like a peach, and it is a great while ripe before the peach trees. But so that the tre be well known, I pase not greatly what name it is knowen by". He seems to have approved of it. It was probably introduced about 1524 by Henry VIII's gardener, Wolf. We read of Pepys visiting a lady and leaving her in her garden "picking apricots to preserve".

At Aynho, a village in Northamptonshire, many of the cottages have apricot trees growing up them, for in 1616 the Lord of the Manor gave his tenants the trees and asked them to pay their tithes in apricots rather than in money, which was probably advantageous to all parties. They do very well in Aynho and it is surprising that more people do not grow them today. John Rea listed 6 different varieties grown in the Restoration period.

To make a Gooseberry Foole

Take your Gooseberries, and put them in a Silver or Earthen Pot, and set it in a Skillet of boyling Water, and when they are coddled enough strain them, then make them hot again when they are scalding hot, beat them very well with a good peece of fresh Butter, Rose-water and Sugar, and put in the yelks of two or three Eggs, you may put Rose-water into them, and so stir it altogether, and serve to the Table when it is cold.

Orchards and fruit gardens were laid out in strict symmetry sometimes walled and sometimes hedged. If they were walled then fruit trees such as peaches, apricots, figs and cherries could be grown up them and given protection from the wind and animals too. We know that John Evelyn had grown at Sayes Court a magnificent holly hedge 400 feet long, 9 feet high and 5 feet in diameter. He wrote:

Is there under Heaven a more glorious and refreshing object of the kind than an impregnable Hedge... at any time of the year, glittering with its armed and varnished leaves? It mocks at the rudest assaults of Weather, Beasts or Hedgebreakers.

Gooseberry bush

Redcurrant Fool

2 tablespoons custard powder
2 tablespoons milk
1/2 pint/275 ml milk
3/4 lb/350 g redcurrants (keep a few for decoration)
1/4 pint/150 ml water
3 tablespoons sugar
1 carton, 5 oz/142 ml double cream

Heat milk and mix up the custard powder in the 2 tablespoons of milk to a smooth paste. Pour boiling milk onto custard powder, stir and return to the pan to cook; it will become very thick. Put on one side. Boil currants in water and sugar until soft, strain through a sieve onto the custard and then liquidize. Let it get cold. Whip cream until almost stiff and then fold the fool into it. It will now be a lovely pink colour so pour it into a glass bowl and decorate with a few raw currants.

Inside these sheltered gardens strawberries and raspberries were cultivated and had been since the time of Tusser in the 1580s, and several kinds of currants and gooseberries. Celia Fiennes when visiting Woburn wrote: "I eate a great quantity of the Red Coraline gooseberry which is a large thin skinned sweet gooseberry".

Sir William Temple after the Restoration lived at Sheen and was very proud of his walled fruit, and thought they were comparable with any in Italy or France. He grew cherries, "Sheen plums", peaches and "standard apricocks". Another gardener noted that Sir William's "wall fruit trees are most exquisitely nail'd and train'd, far better than I ever noted". He had a wide variety and "from the earliest Cherry and Strawberry to the last Apples and Pears may furnish every Day of the circling year".

We know that Henry VIII planted a large cherry orchard of 600 trees and that his daughter Elizabeth was fond of them too. A Jacobean garden was planted with 119 trees, and Tradescant, who was a professional plant and tree collector had 24 different sorts of cherry tree some of which came from Germany.

Sir Kenelm Digby had a recipe for Morello Cherry Wine. The Morello is a bitter cherry which is good for cooking and makes delicious pies or jam. It is well worth having in a garden and will be quite happy on a north facing wall.

CAKES AND BISCUITS

To make a Cake the way of the Royal Princess, the Lady Elizabeth daughter to King Charles the first.

Take half a peck of Flower, half a pinte of Rose-water, a pinte of Ale yest, a pinte of Cream, boyl it, a pound and a half of Butter, six Eggs, (leave out the whites) four pound of Currants, one half pound of Sugar, one Nutmegg and a little Salt, work it very well, and let it stand half an hour by the fire, and then worke it again, and then make it up, and let it stand an hour and a half in the Oven, let not your Oven be too hot.

Princess Elizabeth, Henrietta Maria's fifth child, was born on 29 December 1635 at St. James' Palace. Her mother had ordered a layette, which included a cradle and a bed, costing nearly £2,500. Ambassadors brought presents of "a massy piece of amber greese, two fair and almost transparent China basins, an exquisite clock of curious art, and four admirable pieces", which were paintings by Titian and Tintoretto.

Elizabeth was the only fair-haired member of the family and was always delicate; a gentle little girl with ash blonde ringlets and members of the Court, remembering her birth on Holy Innocents' Day, with snow covering London called her the Winter Princess. She was by far the most scholarly of the Royal children and occupied her rather unhappy and lonely childhood by learning Greek and Hebrew, and was renowned for her attachment to the Protestant religion and reading of theology. Her

Charles I's children

108

Boodles' Club Cake

1 lb/450 g flour
10 oz/275 g soft brown sugar
10 oz/275 g butter
1 lb/450 g raisins
2 eggs
1/2 pint/275 ml milk

Rub the butter into the flour, then add the sugar and raisins. Beat the eggs and add them to the mixture and then add enough milk to make a fairly soft mixture. Put into a prepared cake tin and bake at 325°F (170°C) Gas Mark 3 for 2 hours. Test to see that it is done, then take out of the oven and cool for 5 minutes before turning out onto a wire rack.

lessons were taught by Mrs Makin who was an excellent linguist. By 1642 the country had been plunged into Civil War, and the domestic life of the Royal Family was further disrupted. In 1645 her governess, the Countess of Dorset died and so Elizabeth and her younger brother, Henry, were put into the guardianship of the Earl and Countess of Northumberland and spent that summer at Syon House. Two years later, after a separation of 5 years, Elizabeth was allowed to spend 2 days with her father who was by this time a prisoner at Caversham; after this the King was moved to Hampton Court and could see the 2 children fairly frequently when they stayed at Syon House not far away. Then the King was moved to Carrisbrooke Castle on the Isle of Wight.

Meanwhile James, Duke of York, was being held at St. James's Palace and Elizabeth when she went to St. James's often urged him to escape, and eventually on 20 April 1648 this was effected under the cover of a game of hide and seek. He was dressed in a woman's clothes and smuggled down the river and over the North Sea to Middleburg and Dort and went to stay with his older sister, the Princess of Orange, at the Hague.

On 27 January 1649 sentence was passed on the King and he asked to see the children. They were brought 2 days later to take their last leave, and he was beheaded outside the Banqueting House the next day. Elizabeth was prostrate with grief and her health deteriorated. When Parliament decided that the children should go to Carrisbrooke Elizabeth was horrified at the idea of going to what had been her father's prison. Within less than a week of arriving at Carrisbrooke she went down with a fever and died. A wave of sympathy swept England when it was learned that she had died with her Bible open at the text "come unto me all ye that travail and are heavy laden and I will give ye peace".

Her mother and members of her household remembered that Elizabeth particularly liked this currant cake and included the recipe in the cookery book 6 years later.

To make Almond Jumbolls

Take a pound of Almonds to half a pound of double refined Sugar beaten and Sarced, lay your Almonds in water a day before you Blanch them, and beat them small with your Sugar; and when it is beat very small, put in a handful of Gum-dragon, it being before over night steeped in Rose-water, and half a white of an Egge beaten to froth, and half a spoonful of Coriander seed as many Fennell and Aniseeds, mingle these together very well, set them upon a soft fire till it grows pretty thick, then take it off the fire, and lay it upon a clean Paper, and beat it well with a Rowling pin till it work like a soft Past, and so make them up, and lay them upon papers oyld with oyle of Almons, then put them in your Oven, and so soon as they be throwly risen, take them out before they grow hard.

We know that tarts were made of borage flowers, marigolds, primroses and cowslips, but eggs and curds were added too so the flowers were for flavour and colour rather than for nourishment.

Cowslips were valued as sedatives and were made into syrups that could be kept. They were also dried in the sun and added to tea leaves, partly to eke out the tea which was very expensive, but also to counteract the stimulant quality of the tea if it caused sleeplessness. Gerarde in the 1690s recommended primrose tea to be drunk in May as a cure for the "phrensie", and so one could "minister to a mind diseased". Cowslips were also made into ointment that "taketh away the spots and wrinkles of the skin and doth beautify exceedingly, as divers ladies and gentlewomen, and the citizens, whether wives or widows, know well enough".

Violets were used and appreciated for their rather pungent smell and taste. They were included in a salad: "Take endive, finely curled celery, a sprinkling of chopped parsley, a single olive and the petals of two or three dozen blue violets. Mix these with the purest olive oil, a seasoning of salt and pepper, a dash of Bordeaux and a soupcon of white wine vinegar", and these experiments are to be recommended. "Violet Plate" was a favourite confection of Charles I. "Plate" was really a conserve cut up into pieces rather like lozenges, or "sucking sweetmeats". It was said "it is most pleasant and wholesome and especially it comforteth the heart and inward parts". There are recipes for "plate" in the household book of the Fairfax family which are mostly of sugar with flavourings of amber-gris, violets, roses, marigolds and so on.

Rosewater was used a great deal and is nearly always included when using almonds for it stopped the ground almonds from oiling. Red rose petals appear in many medicinal recipes as well as in cookery. Rose petals were put over cherries in pies before the crust was put on. Conserves were made and rose petal jam. This is still made and used in Greece and in Eastern Europe. One speciality of Poland is a rose petal cake which has a shortbread base, a thick squidgy layer of rose petal conserve and a top of crisp meringue which is absolutely delicious. But the right sort of rose petals have to be used; either the kind used in the perfumery business, or else the very old fashioned pale pink ones with a heady scent.

Flapjack

8 oz/225 g porridge oats
6 oz/175 g butter
6 oz/175 g sugar
2 tablespoons of golden syrup
1 teaspoon black treacle

Melt butter, sugar and syrup in a saucepan and then stir in the oats.

Either well butter a meat tin or line with non-stick baking paper. Pour mixture into the tin and bake in a moderate oven, 350°F (180°C) Gas Mark 4, for about 12–15 minutes when it will be a golden brown and going crispy at the edges. Let it cool in the tin and then cut into squares before it is quite cold.

Damask water was made at home in the Stillroom.

With Damask water made so well
That all the house there of shall smell
As it were Paradise.

Portrait of a lady in a wreath of flowers

To make Shrewsbury Cakes

Take two pound of flower dryed in the Oven and weighed after it is dryed, then put to it one pound of Butter that must be layd an houre or two in Rosewater, so done, pour the Water from the Butter, and put the Butter to the flower with the yelks and whites of five Eggs, two races of Ginger, and three quarters of a pound of Sugar, a little salt, grate your spice and it will be the better, knead all these together till you may rowl the past, then rowl it forth with the top of a bowl, then prick them with a pen made of wood, or if you have a comb that hath not been used, that will do them quickly, and is best to that purpose, so bake them upon pye plates, but not too much in the Oven, for the heat of the plates will dry them very much, after they come forth of the oven, you may cut them without the bowles of what bigness or what fashion you please.

Only three of Henrietta Maria's 9 children survived her and Henrietta Anne only by 9 months. These early deaths were as common as the many pregnancies. The Court would go into mourning and State rooms would be hung with black velvet. Funerals were sometimes occasions of much pomp and ceremony, but sometimes were conducted very quietly and soon after the death, as was the case of the Queen's first baby.

Often funerals took place at night; John Evelyn describes how, as a young man, he followed his father's hearse to the church and there heard a "Sermon and a funebral oration by the Minister", before his father was interred. This was an awesome occasion in midwinter in the dark with only flickering torchlight. His mother had died a few months earlier, and in her last days had asked to see her servants to whom she gave pious instructions. Then she summoned all her children and gave them advice, and a "Ring with her Blessing".

There are accounts for the funeral expenses of an undergraduate who died in 1618 which show the customs of the time:

To the women who laid him out 4/-

For wine etc. for the Schollers that sate up all night with the corse 5/

For candle and perfumes 10d

A man that sate up and fetch all things 1/-

Beer 9d

His coffin 6/8

Before the funeral for the Master and Fellows of the College:

2 pottel of brewed wine and 16 cakes 7/4

Borrowing black clothes for the pulpit and hearse 2/6

Pins for verses 4d

It was customary to pin Latin and Greek verses onto the pall of a scholar.

From Pepys' diary we get glimpses of the customs of the day; he saw the "Duchess of York, in a fine dress of second mourning for her mother, being black, edged

Ginger Biscuits

1 lb/450 g flour

8 oz/225 g brown sugar

8 oz/225 g golden syrup

6 oz/175 g butter (or any fat)

2 teaspoons ginger

Mix the dry ingredients together well.

Melt butter with syrup and then stir in the dry ingredients. Roll out on a floured board and cut into rounds. Put into greased tins and bake in a moderate oven, 350°F (180°C) Gas Mark 4 for about 7 minutes. Cool on a wire rack before putting in a tin.

This recipe makes a large quantity and if the mixture gets too cool to handle easily while you are cutting out then reheat the pan gently so that the mixture becomes warm and manageable.

with ermine". "This day I was invited to have gone to my Cozen Mary Pepys' buriel, but could not". Invitation cards to funerals could be bought at stationers and sent out to relations and friends. Gloves and ribbons were often given to the pall bearers, and at one funeral Pepys arranged that the servants had white gloves to wear while serving at the funeral party. Many more people came to the party than were invited so he was a little put out to find about 150 instead of 120. They were each given 6 biscuits and "Burnt claret".

From the twelfth until the nineteenth century a custom occasionally observed was to bury a deceased person's heart separately from the rest of the body. During his retirement Izaak Walton lived with his married daughter in the Cathedral Close at Winchester, and when his much loved little granddaughter died her heart in a little lead coffin was buried in the huge flint wall surrounding the garden where she had played.

Funeral invitation

To make Buttered Loaves

Take the yolks of twelve Eggs, and six whites, and a quarter of a pint of yeast, when you have beaten the Eggs well, strein them with the yeast into a Dish, then put to it a little salt, and two rases of Ginger beaten very small, then put flower to it till it come to a high Past that will not cleave, then you must rowle it upon your hands, and afterwards put it into a warme Cloth, and let it lye there a quarter of an houre, then make it up in little Loaves, bake it, against it is baked prepare a pound and half of Butter, a quarter of a pint of white-wine, and half a pound of Sugar; This being melted and beaten together Butter with it, and set them in the Oven a quarter of an hour.

Charlotte de la Tremouille came to England to marry young Lord Strange, the son and heir of Lord Derby. She had a large dowry and was 7 years older than her 17 year-old bridegroom, though that was not admitted at the time. They stayed at Court and she was a friend for the Queen for a while, but unfortunately Lord Strange detested court life and so as soon as Charlotte was pregnant he insisted that they should retire to the country where they lived quietly at either Knowsley or Latham House in Lancashire. They had 9 children. Later, as Countess of Derby, she held one of her husband's houses against siege by the Parliamentarian troops.

During the Civil War she had remained with her children at Latham House when her husband joined the King. Lancashire favoured the Parliamentary cause and by May 1643 Latham House was the only place held by the King's adherents. The following year on 28 February Sir William Fairfax laid siege and the Countess, after a week of parleys, refused to surrender declaring that she and her children would set fire to the castle and die rather than yield. On 2O March 2 of her messengers got through the enemy lines and conveyed urgent appeals for help to Prince Rupert and the Earl of Derby. On 1O April the Parliamentarians brought up a new mortar which threatened to put an end to the defence, but at about 4 o'clock on the morning of 22 April, the garrison made a dashing sortie and captured the mortar. This disheartened the besiegers and on 26 May Prince Rupert and his troops arrived from Newark and the Parliamentarians withdrew to Bolton. The Prince stormed Bolton and sent the Countess a present of the 22 banners which had recently waved over the heads of her besiegers. The Earl escorted his wife and children to the Isle of Man and there she stayed until after the execution of her husband in 1651.

Years later there is a charming letter from the Countess to her sister-in-law in Paris asking a favour. Would one of her waiting women kindly do a little shopping for her; she wanted "a French doll; the most beautiful to be had, that will undress. It is for a little girl whose parents I greatly wish to oblige".

Ginger Crunch

4 oz/50 g butter
4 oz/50 g sugar
7 oz/200 g flour
1 teaspoon ginger

Icing

2 tablespoons golden syrup
2 tablespoons butter
4 tablespoons icing sugar
1 teaspoon ginger

Cream butter and sugar and then add the flour and ginger; knead well and press down hard into a greased shallow tin. Bake in a moderately hot oven at 375°F (190°C) Gas Mark 5 for 15–20 minutes.

Meanwhile put the ingredients for the icing in a pan and heat until it is all melted and smooth. Take the biscuit out of the oven and immediately pour the hot icing over it, tilting the tin to get the icing into the corners. Leave to cool and then cut into squares before it is quite cold.

The Countess was at the Palace of Whitehall to welcome back Henrietta Maria after 19 years abroad. Old friends crowded the Palace and Lady Derby wrote with mingled joy and sorrow that her Majesty's arrival took place amid "the acclamations of the whole nation. I saw her and kissed her hand. She met me with much emotion and received me with tears and great kindness. You may imagine what I felt. Her Majesty charms all who see her and her courtesy cannot be praised enough".

Dolls owned by Lord and Lady Clapham

To Make a Marchpan; to Ice him, &c

Take two pound of Almonds blanched, and beaten in a stone Morter till they begin to come to a fine Past, and take a pound of sifted Sugar, and put it in the Morter with the Almonds, and so leave it till it come to a perfect Past, putting in now and then a Spoonful of Rosewater to keep them from Oyling; when you have beaten them to a perfect Past cover the Marchpan in a sheet, as big as a Charger, and set an edge about as you do about a Tart, and a bottom of wafers under him; thus bake it in an oven or baking pan, when you see your marchpan is hard and dry, take it out and Ice him with Rosewater and sugar being made as thick as butter for Fritters, so spread it on him with a wing-fether, so put it into the Oven again, and when you see it rise high, then take it out and garnish it with some prety conceits made part of the same stuff, stick long cumfets upright in him, so serve it.

In very early mythology it was thought that the bees carried the delicate filement of life, or soul, back to the country where as Virgil says "there is no room for death and where the souls fly free, ranging the heavens to join the stars, imperishable number".

There has always been a very close link between the bees and the bee-keeper's household. It was a common practice, and may still be in use, to tell the bees if a death occurred in the family. The beekeeper would go to the hive after sunset and pin a piece of black crepe on it, then gently tap the hive and tell the bees who it was who had died. It was thought that if you did not tell the bees, they would leave or else pine away and die too.

Old beekeepers would always talk gently to their bees and never shout or swear at them; they were treated with great courtesy and then they did not get angry. It was thought that the bees knew their beekeeper's voice and also his own particular smell, and it was advisable to avoid eating onions or garlic before handling a swarm. In previous centuries the "wisdom of the bees" was a very real belief.

In old records of people's wills as well as land, houses, furniture, often beds, books and jewellery, hives are often itemised. In 1584 William Styleman, yeoman, left 6 of 10 hives of bees to his maidservant and one to his Vicar; a Romford man left "to my dame a swarm of bees I have at Noak Hill". They were never sold for money but given away on the subtle understanding that the recipient would in due course repay in goods or a service. They were very highly prized and in the Isle of Man a law was passed in 1629 making it a capital offence to steal a hive of bees.

Honey was a valuable ingredient of cooking being the main source of sweeetening till the sugar plantations in the West Indies were fully developed. It is interesting to note that in 1580 honey cost 3 pence a pound and sugar 17 pence a pound, and it was not until 1800 that parity was reached, and after that sugar became cheaper than honey. The wax was used for making good quality candles, for ointments, and for polishes for wood and leather.

Gingerbread

8 oz/225 g golden syrup
1 dessertspoon black treacle
4 oz/125 g sugar
4 oz/125 g butter
1/4 pint/150 ml milk
8 oz/225 g flour
4 oz/125 g sultanas (if liked)
1 teaspoon ginger
1/2 teaspoon mixed spice
1/2 level teaspoon bicarbonate of soda
1 egg

Put syrup, treacle, sugar, butter and milk in a saucepan and melt. When cool add the beaten egg. Mix the dry ingredients and stir into the mixture. Pour into a well buttered meat-tin and bake in a cool oven, 300°F (150°C) Gas Mark 2, for an hour or more. Test, and let it rest for about 10 minutes before cutting into squares and lifting onto a wire rack.

Bees were not to be found in America and so hives were taken out and there is a letter dated 5 December 1621 from the Council of the Virginia Company in London saying "We have by this ship (either the Bona Nova or the Hopewell) and the Discovery sent you divers sorte of seed, and fruit trees, as also pidgeons, connies (rabbits), Peacocke Mastiffs (watch dogs), and bee hives". The bees were called the "whiteman's flies" by the American Indians

Catching the swarm

To make Almond Cakes

Take half a pound of Almonds blanched in cold Water, beat them with some Rose-water till they do not Glister, then they will be beaten; if you think fit, lay seven or eight Musque Comfits dissolved in Rosewater which must not be above six or seven spoonfulls for fear of spoiling the colour, when they be thus beaten, put in half a pound of Sugar finely sifted, beat them and the Almonds together till it be well mixed, then take the whites of two Eggs and two spoonfulls of fine flour that hath been dried in an Oven, beat these well together and poure it to your Almonds, then butter your Plates and dust your Cakes with Sugar and Flower, and when they are a little brown, draw them, and when the Oven is colder set them in again on brown Papers, and they will look whiter.

Honey was often used in the preparation of both food and drink. Huge quantities were used each year in the making of mead and methaglin. We know that "Lady Hungerford who useth to make her mead at the end of the summer when she takes up her honey, and begins to drink it in Lent". Hartman writes:

Metheglin is esteemed to be a very wholesome Drink; and doubtless it is so, since all the world consents that Honey is a precious substance being the choice and collection which Bees made of the most pure, most delectable, and most odoriferous parts of plants, more particularly of their flowers and fruits. Metheglin is therefore esteemed to be an excellent Pectoral, good against Consumption and Asthma – it is cleansing and diuretic, good against the stone, it is restorative and strengthening, it comforts and strengthens the Noble parts, and affords good nourishment being made good use of by the Healthy as well as by the Sick.

The Feminine Monarchy, a book on bees was written by Charles Butler and published in 1609. He was vicar of Wooton St.Lawrence for 47 years and had studied his bees very carefully. He worked out that the worker bees were the female and the drones male. He realized that the Queen ruled the hive but had not come to the conclusion that she was the mother. The book was very successful and out of the profits he was able to give his daughter whom he referred to as his "sweet honey girl" a dowry of £400.

Bee hives were simple domes of plaited straw or willow twigs but experiments were being made and new forms of bee management were being tried. John Evelyn writing in his diary in 1654 records how he dined at Oxford with:

That most obliging and universaly Curious Dr. Wilkins, at Waddum, who was the first who shew'd me the Transparant Apiaries, which he had built like Castle and Palaces and so ordered them one upon another, as to take the Honey without destroying the Bees,… and he so abundantly civill, as finding me pleased with them, to present me one of these Hives, which he had empty, and which I afterwards had in my garden at Says-Court many years after; and which his Majestie came on purpose to see and contemplate with much satisfaction.

Macaroons

4 oz/125 g ground almonds
6 oz/185 g castor sugar
2 egg whites
$^1/_2$ oz/15 g cornflour
2 teaspoons water
Almonds to decorate
Rice paper

Put ground almonds, castor sugar and egg whites into a bowl and beat for 1 minute then add cornflour and water and beat again. Put the rice paper on baking sheets and put spoonfuls of the mixture on it but leave enough room for them to spread a little. Bake in a moderately hot oven 325°F (170°C) Gas Mark 3 for about 15 minutes until they are a golden brown. They should be crisp all round the outside and just soft in the centre. Let them cool and trim off the excess rice paper.

Pepys in 1665 wrote:

After dinner to Mr Evelyn's, he being abroad, we walked in his garden and a lovely noble ground he hath indeed. Among other rareities a hive of bees, so as being hived in glass you may see the bees making their honey and combs mightily pleasantly.

It was obviously very novel and intriguing.

A new mode of beehive

CAKES AND BISCUITS

To make Italian Biskets

Take a quarter of a pound of searsed Sugar, and beat it in an Alabaster Mortar with the white of an Egge, and a little Gum Dragon steept in Rose-water, to bring it to a perfect paste, then mould it up with a little Anniseed and a grain of Musk; then make it up like Dutch bread, and bake it in a Pye plate in a warm Oven, till they rise somewhat high and white, take them out, but handle them not till they be throughly dry and cold.

The first day of May was a day for festivities and merrymaking and there were many old customs and superstitions. Young girls would go out into the meadows at dawn and wash their faces in dew as it was thought to have beautifying qualities on this special morning.

We know that the Queen organized a Maying expedition one year and a large number of lords and ladies in 150 coaches set out for the country. When she saw a May tree in full bloom she got out and picked some to decorate her hat.

Hone's *Table Book* tells of a May day custom in the village of Ranwick in Gloucestershire:

There has been from time immemorial a custom that three large cheeses decked with the gayest flowers are placed in litters, also decorated with flowers and bows of trees waving at the corners. They are thus borne through the village accompanied by a joyous throng, shouting and huzzaaring with all their might and main, and usually accompanied by a little band of music. They proceed in this manner to the church yard where the cheeses being taken from the litters and divested of their floral ornaments, are rolled three times round the church. They are then carried back in the same state, and in the midst of the village are cut up and distributed piecemeal to the inhabitants.

During the Commonwealth period such customs were suppressed and May poles and dancing were forbidden. In Hone's book there is this poem:

In London thirty years ago
When milkmaids went about
It was a goodly sight to see
Their May day pageant all drawn out.
Such scenes and sounds once blest my eyes
And charmed my ears; but all have vanish'd
On May day now no garlands go,
For milkmaids and their dance are banish'd.

However, the old customs did not die for Samuel Pepys records seeing in 1667, the milkmaids dancing before the houses of their customers:

Thence to Westminster, in the way meeting many milkmaids with their garlands upon their pails, dancing with a fiddler before them; and saw pretty Nelly (Nell Gwyn) standing at her lodgings' door in Drury Lane in her smock sleeves and bodice, looking upon one; she seemed a mighty pretty creature.

Moist Orange Cake

8 oz/225 g flour

5 oz/150 g sugar

3 1/2 oz/80 g butter

2 large oranges

2 eggs

Butter icing

4 oz/125 g butter

8 oz/225 g icing sugar

1 tablespoon of orange juice

Rub the butter into the flour and then add the sugar. Beat the eggs; grate the rind off the oranges and squeeze out the juice.Gradually add the eggs to the butter and flour, and then add the orange juice and rind. Pour into prepared tin. Bake in a moderately hot oven at 400°F (200°C) Gas Mark 6 for about 35 minutes and then test. Remove from the oven and let the cake rest for a few minutes before turning out on to a rack.

When cold ice with butter icing or cut the cake in half and put the icing in the middle. Beat the butter till pale and gradually beat in the icing sugar and orange juice; spread over the cake. Alternatively ice with ordinary icing made of icing sugar and orange juice; this is a good cake for a child's birthday cake. There is no need to ice it as it is very delicious plain.

Brass tablet in Wells Cathedral showing a pious gentleman who had given up his plumed hat, dice, sword, tennis racket and viol.

To make Cracknels

Take halfe a pound of fine flower, dryed and searced, as much fine Sugar searced, mingled with a spoonfull of Corriander seed bruised, half a quarter of a pound of Butter rubbed in the flower and Sugar, then wet it with the yelks of two Eggs, and half a spoonful of white Rose-water, a spoonful or little more of Cream as will wet it, knead the Past till it be soft and limber to rowle well, then rowle it extreame thin and cut them round by little plates, lay them upon buttered papers, and when they go into the Oven, prick them, and wash the Top with the yelk of an Egge beaten and made thin with Rose-water or faire water they will give with keeping, therefore before they are eaten, they must be dryed in a warm Oven to make them crisp.

Games featured largely in seventeenth-century life as there were few books and books were expensive. Outdoor games provided social occasions as well as exercise.

In one city the surveyor was ordered to select a suitable site "for merchants and gentlemen to recreate themselves on at bowles", and so a space was enclosed as a bowling green and subsequently brought in a good rental. We know that years earlier Sir Francis Drake played bowls on Plymouth Hoe while waiting for the Armada to sail up the English Channel, and that he finished his game after the Spanish ships had been sighted. Many of the large country houses had their own bowling greens. Another popular game for the gentlemen was tennis and Henry VIII had a Court built at Whitehall. But one mother wrote anxiously to her son at University and told him to "beware of violent tennisinge or leapinge or any other thinge which shall hinder your healthe". Shuttlecock and battledore were both played a good deal and sometimes they were played in tennis courts and became very violent. The people of Williton, a village in Somerset, had to be ordered not to play "tenez" up against the church walls, but some years later had to be reprimanded again and asked to cease playing Fives there. Fives is a game that originated at Eton, the boys using their hands not a racket, hitting the ball up against corner walls. They also invented the Eton Wall Game which is still played at the school today.

At times of festivals dancing round the Maypole was enjoyed by country people, and girls did country dancing together. The nursery rhyme Ring-a-ring-a-roses, A pocketful of posies, Atishoo, Atishoo, We all fall down, dates back to the days of the plague. Posies of sweet smelling herbs were thought to fend off the disease, and sneezing was one of the first symptoms of plague.

Morris dancers, always men, formed themselves into bands and went round and danced at local fairs and festivals. We can read of one irate parson in 1634 complaining bitterly "that on Midsomer day last in the time of Morning Prayer and sermon a company from Gallington and other places came with a Morrice Daunce and with Fidlers and with a drume, and held on theire sports so neere the Church". He asked them to "to leafe makeing such a noise", but to no avail.

In the new royal parks, the Spring Garden by Whitehall, and the New Garden at Vauxhall, people could walk and play games after the Puritan ban on games was lifted; games such as football, skittles, quoits and a kind of cricket.

Sandwich biscuits

4 oz/125 g butter

2 oz/50 g sugar

3 oz/75 g plain flour

3 oz/75 g self raising flour

pinch of salt

yolk of one egg

apricot jam

icing sugar

lemon juice

Sift both flours and salt together. Beat butter and sugar to a cream and add egg yolk. Gradually work in the flour so it forms a soft dough. Roll out on a floured board and cut into circles. Place on a greased baking tray and bake in a slow oven 300°F (150°C) Gas Mark 2 for about 15 minutes until just pale brown. Cool on a wire rack.

Spread half the biscuits with apricot jam. Mix up a little icing sugar with some lemon juice and put a blob on each remaining biscuit. Sandwich biscuits in pairs. Alternatively spread with chocolate spread and put on a blob of chocolate icing.

Aristocratic games were fencing, tennis, golf and Pell Mell. Pell Mell had come over from France and was a forerunner of croquet but more energetic and dangerous. It was played on the ground which is now Pall Mall.

Samuel Pepys and his friends while travelling in a wagon played Crambo which is described as "a play at short verses in which a word is given, and the parties contend to find most rhymes to it". This would be a good car game today for long journeys.

The Thames at Richmond

To make fine Pan-cakes fryed without Butter or Lard

Take a pint of Creame, and six new laid Eggs, beat them very well together, put in a quarter of a pound of Sugar, and one Nutmeg, or a little beat Mace (which you please) and so much flowre as will thicken, almost as much as ordinary Pan-cake batter, your Pan must be heated reasonably hot and wiped with a clean Cloth; this done put in your Batter as thick or thin as you please.

The main part of a large meal was taken in the Great Hall or a smaller dining chamber, but some of the large houses had special banqueting rooms as well. At this time the banquet was the sweet course, or dessert, that followed a large feast.

The guests moved out of the dining chamber and walked to the banquet, which was informal and intimate. These banqueting rooms were often several small rooms, or Gazebos in the garden but quite close to the house, or in turrets on the roof. At Longleat for example Sir John Thynne had built a number of little domed banqueting turrets, some octagonal and some square with windows looking out over the gardens and countryside. They would only have room for about 5 or 6 people and for a small central table. So the guests would walk to and fro informally on the 'leads' of the roof from one turret to another to meet their friends and look at the view. Drinks would have been served and pretty confections such as tarts, jellies, syllabubs and so on.

In Gervaise Markham's book *The English Housewife* (1615), he gives a list of suitable things to serve on such an occasion which include cinnamon water, wormwood water and ipocras to drink, and what we would now term "finger food" to eat. He suggests gingerbread, which was probably gilded prettily, jumbles, Banbury cakes, marzipan, marmalade, quince cakes and quince paste and suckets. All rather special and pretty party food in those days of expensive sugar.

Many of them we still have as party or Christmas fare, but some cannot be obtained unless made at home. Quince paste is to be recommended and is very simply quinces and a large cooking apple peeled and cored, sliced and boiled with sugar until it is a very thick seething mass. By this time it will have become a lovely golden red colour. Then pour it into a buttered dish and cut into cubes when it is cold; it is a bit sticky but delicious.

Teatime Pancakes

6 oz/175 g flour
3 oz/75 g sugar
1 egg
1/3 pint/200 ml milk
1/4 teaspoon salt
Lard for frying

Beat the egg and sugar till thick, add salt and then beat in milk and flour alternately (or liquidize all together). Put a very little lard in a non-stick frying pan and heat; spoon in pools of the batter; let it cook for a minute or two and then turn over to brown the other side.

Either eat hot out of the pan or cool on a tray and then spread with butter.

Children enjoy making these pancakes and can dribble the batter into the pan to form their own initials, or to make animal shapes.

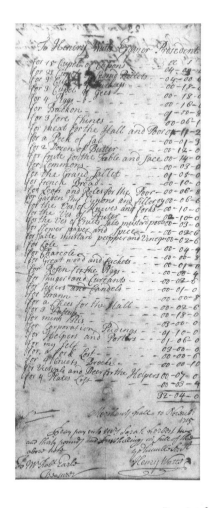 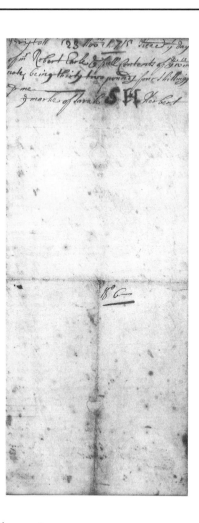

Receipt for a banquet

To make Mrs. Leeds Cheese Cakes

Take six quarts of milk and ren it prety cold, and when it is tender come, drayn from it your Whey in a strayner, then hang it up till all the whey be dropt from it, then presse it, change it into dry cloaths till it wet the cloth no longer, then beat it in a stone Morter, till it be like Butter, then strayne it through a thin strayner, mingle it with a pound and a half of Butter with your hands, take one pound of Almonds, and beat them with Rosewater till they are like your Curd, then mingle them with the yelks of twenty Eggs and a quart of Cream, two great nutmegs, one pound and half of Sugar, when your Coffins are ready and going to set in the Oven then mingle them together, let your Oven be made hot enough for a Pigeon Pye, and let a stone stand up till the scorching be past, then set them in, half an hour will bake them well, your Coffins must be made with Milk and Butter as stiffe as for other Past then you must set them into a pretty hot Oven, and fill them full of Bran, and when they are harded, take them out, and with a Wing brush out the Bran, they must be pricked.

The parish was the unit both of the Church and State and had its own structure to look after law and order and social needs. The church wardens were responsible for the relief of the poor and for the upkeep of the fabric of the church. The parish clerk rang the bell for services, set out the Bible and prayerbook and made arrangements for communions and baptisms. He wore a surplice and led the congregation in the responses of the public prayers.

The sexton was entitled to certain dues at Christmas and Easter as well as fees which he was allowed to charge for digging graves. In the vestry book at Houghton there is the following entry:

James Dobson of Houghton is to continue in his father's plaice as Sexton, and to haive the dues belonging to the plaice as it appears by an order sett downe in this book — that is two pence or bunns at Christmas, and eggs at Easter, for a grave in the churchyard two pence, in the church four pence, in the quire six pence.

He was responsible for cleaning the church, lighting fires and the general charge of the building.

The beadle was expected to help the constable in apprehending and punishing rogues. He wore a special dress and carried a whip, or wand, with which he drove dogs out of church. It was his duty to tell people of parish meetings and in some places he acted as town crier. A pair of stocks was maintained in every parish for the punishment of drunkards and others.

Many churches had a peal of bells which were rung before services, or tolled for the dead. Change ringing in unique to England and is very skilled with the Master of the Tower calling the changes to his team of ringers. The Puritans during the Commonwealth forbade the ringing of church bells, but the art soon flourished again. During this time in 1658 the Bellringers at Halstead in Essex had a great

Walnut Cake with Frosting

8 oz/225 g flour
4 oz/125 g butter
8 oz/225 g castor sugar
Pinch of salt
$^1/_2$ teaspoon vanilla essence
2 eggs
4 oz/125 g walnuts (keep 6 halves for decoration)
$^1/_4$ pint/150 ml milk

Frosting
8 oz/225 g sugar
1 egg white
$^1/_8$ pint/75 ml water

Prepare cake tin. Chop walnuts. Separate one egg.

Beat butter till creamy, beat in sugar and vanilla, add egg and egg yolk. Stir in walnuts and add flour and enough milk to make a soft consistency. Pour into prepared cake tin and bake in moderate oven 350°F (180°C) Gas Mark 4 for about 30 minutes, then test. Turn out onto a wire rack and when cold make icing.

Lightly whisk egg white in a large bowl. Dissolve sugar in the water and bring to the boil and continue boiling until it reaches 240°F (120°C). Holding the pan high above the bowl slowly pour the sugar onto the egg white (much easier with 2 people) and beat all the time. The mixture will become opaque with beating and will leave a thick trail from the whisk. Pour the thick frosting quickly over the cake and spread down the sides. Decorate with walnut halves and leave to set for $^1/_2$ hour.

Ringers' jar made which would hold 4$^1/_2$ gallons of ale. On it are the initials of the five ringers and the verse:

Be merry and wise
Use me much and break me not
For I am but an earthen pot
As we sit by the fire to keepe ourselves warme
This pot of good liquor will do us no harme
If you be wise
Fil me not twice
At one sitting
In summer heate
And winter cold
To drink of this
We dare be bold.

CAKES AND BISCUITS

> ## To make a very good
> ## Great Oxfordshire Cake
>
> *Take a peck of flower by weight, and dry it a little, and a pound and a half of Sugar, one ounce of Cinamon, half a ounce of Nutmeg, a quarter of an ounce of mace and Cloves, a good spoonfull of Salt, beat your Salt and spice very fine, and searce it, and mix it with your flower and Sugar, then take three pound of Butter, and work it in the flower, it will take two hours working, then take a quart of Ale yeast, two quarts of Cream, halfe a pint of Sack, six grains of Amber-greece dissolved in it, halfe a pinte of Rosewater, sixteen Eggs, eight of the Whites, mix these with the flour and knead them well together, then let it lye warm by the fire till your Oven be hot; which must be a little hotter then for manchet, when you make it ready for your Oven, put to your Cake six pound of Currants, two pound of Raisons of the Sun stoned and minced, so make up your Cake, and set it in your oven stopped close, it wil take three hours a baking, when baked, take it out and frost it over with the white of an Egg and Rosewater, well beat together, and strew fine Sugar upon it, and then set it again into the Oven that it may Ice.*

Tobacco was cultivated after its introduction into England in 1583, and it proved a considerable source of income to the inhabitants of Gloucestershire until the trade was placed under restrictions. There is a tract written by a disgruntled hangman:

The very planting of tobacco have proved the decay of my trade, for since it hath been planted in Gloucestershire, especially at Winchcomb, my trade hath proved nothing worth. Then 'twas a merry world with me, for indeed before tobacco was there planted, there being no kind of trade to employ men and very small tillage, necessity compelled poor men to stand my friends by stealing sheep and other cattel, breaking of hedges, robbing of orchards, and what not.

So with the prosperity brought by the growing of tobacco the hangman had no criminals to hang.

Poor people who could not afford the long clay pipes made rudimentary pipes out of walnut shells and straws. In Malmesbury market men bought tobacco by the shillingworth, weighing the tobacco in the scales against their shilling and so they stored up new, unworn shillings to use when buying their tobacco so getting the most possible weight.

The cultivation was first prohibited during the Commonwealth and more Acts were passed in the reign of Charles II. The Government declared that the import of tobacco was a monopoly for the benefit of London merchants and customs duty on this import should be paid in London. However, the arbitrary order had to be withdrawn because so many of the ships coming from America pretended damage and put into small ports in Devon, Dorset and Cornwall. The tobacco cargo was then alleged to have been damaged or lost, when in fact it was smuggled ashore and so no duty was paid. The Government had to reverse their policy and give the right of import to Southampton, Dartmouth, Plymouth and Bristol.

Date Cake

8 oz/225 g dates

1 teaspoon bicarbonate of soda

8 oz/225 g brown sugar

3 oz/75 g butter

Pinch of salt

10 oz/275 g flour

1 egg

1 teaspoon vanilla essence

2 oz/50 g chopped walnuts

Optional Icing

5 tablespoons brown sugar

2 tablespoons butter

2 tablespoons cream or milk

Put bicarbonate of soda into 1 cup of boiling water and add chopped dates. Cream butter and sugar and add beaten egg, add flour, vanilla and a generous pinch of salt. Add the date mixture and beat, add walnuts. Line a baking tin, about 7 in. x 11 in. and pour the mixture in. Bake in a moderate oven 350°F (180°C) Gas Mark 4, for about 20 minutes, test. Allow to cool a little before turning out onto a rack to get cold.

To make icing, heat all together in a pan until the sugar is dissolved and then boil for about 17 minutes to reach the soft-ball stage when a drop is dropped into a cup of cold water. Cool a little and then beat until it begins to granulate; quickly pour over the cake and leave to set.

A Dutch traveller to Gloucester noted the prevalence of tobacco smoking:

Supper being finished they set on the table half a dozen pipes, and a packet of tobacco for smocking, which is a general custom amoungst women as well as men, who think that without tobacco one cannot live in England, because they say it dissipates the humours of the brain.

He goes on to allege that smoking was common amongst schoolboys in Gloucester. A Swiss gentleman was very surprised and shocked to see clergymen in London sitting in coffee houses and inns with long pipes in their mouths.

Broad Street, Bristol

To make Sugar Cakes or Jumballs

Take two pound of flower, dry it and season it very fine, then take a pound of Loaf sugar, and beat it very fine, and searce it, mingle your Flower and Sugar very well, then take a pound and a half of sweet Butter and wash out the Salt, and break it into bits with your Flower and Sugar, then take yelks of four new laid Eggs, and four or five Spoonful of Sack, and four Spoonful of Cream, beat all these together, then put them into your Flower, and knead them to a Past, and make them into what fashion you please, and lay them upon Paper or Plates and put them into the Oven, and be careful of them, for a very little thing bakes them.

Between 1619 and 1631 Thomas Hutchins ran the first profitable postal system which was between London and Plymouth. He was Postmaster at Crewkerne in Somerset which was a regular post stage. There were numerous inns in the town which had 54 guest beds and stabling for 130 horses.

During the Civil War communications in the country must have been very difficult for ordinary people, and it was not until a few years afterwards that a form of postal service on a national scale was established. Charles II saw the necessity of this and helped its development. He proclaimed a post between London and Edinburgh to go and come back in 6 days, and this was to take "all such letters as shall be directed to any post town in or near the road". We know that some years later Daniel Defoe sent a letter 80 miles for 2 pence.

With the restoration of peace and the upsurge of a new wealthy class many large houses in the country were built, and this also helped to increase the demand for a postal service. Because more people were writing letters there began a demand for a piece of furniture to be designed for this purpose. Writing desks had been made for institutions such as monasteries or Colleges, but often in the form of a cupboard with a sloping top to act as the writing desk, usually in oak. Or students had a small portable desk which was a box with a sloping lid which could be put on a table and used for writing on or for placing a book on; papers and books could be kept inside the box.

Now people wanted something to use in their homes. With the advent of the use of dovetailing in furniture making drawers became lighter and easier to make. The result of the demand was the creation of the escritoire or bureau. At first this was the top half of the bureau as we know it today on a stand. The large panel would let down and provide a surface on which to write, and inside would be pigeon-holes in which to keep paper, household accounts and correspondence. Later the chest of drawers bottom half was added making it a most useful piece of furniture.

By the end of the century some bureaux were being made with the addition of a bookcase on top of the bureau, and sometimes the central panel of the door would be of mirror. When made by skilled craftsmen this was a really elegant piece of furniture.

Chocolate Vanilla Cake

5 oz/150 g butter

5 oz/150 g sugar

3 eggs

7 oz/200 g flour

1/2 teaspoon baking powder

1/2 teaspoon vanilla essence

A little milk

Butter icing

4 oz/125 g butter

6 oz/175 g icing sugar

1 heaped tablespoon cocoa

Glace icing

8 oz/225 g icing sugar

1 heaped tablespoon cocoa

Cream the butter and sugar until light and then beat in the eggs one at a time, beat well. Gradually beat in the flour, baking powder and vanilla and enough milk to make it a soft dropping consistency. Pour the mixture into 2 greased and floured straight sided tins and bake in a fairly hot oven at 375°F (190°C) Gas Mark 5 for about 35 minutes. Test, take out and leave to stand for a few minutes before turning out onto a rack to get cold.

Make the butter icing by pouring about 1 dessertspoonful of boiling water onto the cocoa and mix together with the butter and icing sugar. Spread it on one of the cakes and put the other cake on top.

Put about 6 oz/175 g of icing sugar in a bowl. Put the cocoa in a cup and add 2 tablespoons of boiling water and stir this into the icing sugar. Mix the other 2 oz/50 g icing sugar with a little water to get a spreading consistency. Ice the cake all over with the chocolate icing, and then with a spatula take the white icing and swirl it on the top of the cake in a spiral pattern.

Bible box

To make Mrs.Shellyes Cake

Take a peck of fine flower, and three pound of the best Butter, work your flower and butter very well together, then take ten Eggs, leave out six whites, a pint and a half of Ale yeast beat the Eggs and yeast together, and put them to the flower, take six pound of blanched Almonds, beat them very well, puting in sometime Rose-water to keep them from Oyling, adde what Spice you please, let this be put to the rest with half a pint of Sack, and a little Saffron; and when you have made all this into Past, cover it warme before the fire, and let it rise for half an hour, then put in twelve pound of Currants well washed and dryed, two pound of Raisins of the Sun stoned and cut small, one pound of Sugar; the sooner you put it into the Oven after the fruit is put in, the better.

Most furniture was made of wood grown locally, as transport of wood was difficult, and most English trees grow large enough to provide planks of sufficient size for the making of furniture. These trees would be ash, elm, chestnut, sycamore, birch, maple, walnut and oak; but oak was by far the most durable and least prone to rot or attack by woodworm or other beetles as it is very hard. Preparing the wood was a long process; it was soaked in water for a year and then left to dry out slowly for 2 or 3 years before being cut into planks, and then the planks had to be left to season for a year or more depending on their thickness, before being used.

When the tree trunk was ready to be cut into planks it would be pulled across a specially constructed saw-pit. Men who were sawyers worked in pairs and travelled round the country from one estate to another as required doing this very skilled work. One man would stand in the bottom of the pit and one on the top using a long two-handled saw – it was very hard work and needed considerable skill to keep the planks straight and even. The irregular marks left by a pit saw can often be seen on the underside of an old piece of furniture from this period. So "country pieces" as they are called today were made locally all over England and were often a decade or two behind the fashion in London. Usually most really skilled furniture and cabinet-makers gravitated to London.

The making of furniture up to the early seventeenth century was fairly simple and the pieces of wood were joined together with the mortise and tenon joint; the mortise is a rectangular hole cut in one piece of wood and the tenon is a tongue cut in the other piece of wood so that they can slot together. Nails at this time were, of course, hand-made and were inclined to split the wood, or rust, so often wooden pegs were used instead.

Cherry and Almond Cake

8 oz/225 g flour

3 eggs

8 oz/225 g castor sugar

8 oz/225 g butter

4 oz/125 g ground almonds

4 oz/125 g glacé cherries (chopped)

1/2 teaspoon of almond essence

Cream butter and sugar until light and fluffy and then add eggs separately. Gradually add flour, almonds, cherries and almond essence.

Pour into a prepared cake-tin and bake in a cool oven, 300°F (150°C) Gas Mark 2 for about 2 1/2 hours. Test to see that it is done, let it rest for a few minutes before turning out onto a wire rack. This cake is moist and keeps well.

So most tables, stools, benches, beds, cradles, coffers and later cupboards were made in this way, until the technique of dovetailing was developed. Dovetailing was a great improvement and so much less clumsy than the mortise and tenon construction, and with dovetailing much narrower planks could be used. This had a great effect and drawers became much easier and less heavy to make and so the making of chests of drawers became widespread. The dovetailing on the front of a drawer was hidden by moulding. This became possible as glues became better at this time, and these stronger glues also made it possible to use veneers; thin slices of another wood stuck on to the outside visible parts of a piece of furniture, top, front and sides of a chest of drawers for instance. So a large area could be covered with a more expensive high quality wood.

A joint stool

To make Bisket Bread

Take a pound of Sugar fearced very fine, and a pound of flower well dryed, and twelve Eggs, a handful of Carroway-seed, six whites of Eggs, a very little Salt, beat all these together, and keep them with beating till you set them in the Oven, then put them into your Plates, or Tin things and take Butter and put into a Cloth and rub your Plate, a spoonfull into a Plate, is enough, and so set them in the Oven, and let your Oven be no hotter then to bake small-Pyes; if your flower be not dried in the Oven before, they will be heavy.

Small numbers of protestants from France, or Huguenots as they came to be called, were immigrating to England during this century, and Charles II took what general measures he could on behalf of these refugees. Some came with money and valuables but some only escaped with their lives. He ordered a brief to be read in all churches appealing for funds, and granted them Letters of Denization, which conferred a restricted form of British nationality. Some of them were men of ability and were skilled craftsmen such as weavers, glass-makers, cabinet-makers, silver-and goldsmiths, and so they brought with them the knowledge of their trades and different techniques and new designs.

Then in 1685 the Edict of Nantes was revoked by Louis XIV: it had given a measure of toleration to the Huguenots and this revocation forced them to leave France in large numbers and settle in America, the Netherlands and England. Three years later William III came to the throne and brought with him from Holland his architect, David Morot, and a number of skilled craftsmen many of whom were Huguenots. They worked for the King and for members of the Court and created an upsurge of interest in new ideas, new fashions and new designs.

Walnut dining chair

Cassia Biscuits

6 oz/175 g plain flour
3 oz/75 g castor sugar
3 oz/75 g butter
1 oz/25 g currants
1 egg yolk
oil of cassia to taste

Oil of cassia can be bought at health-food stores or sometimes at a chemist.

Cream the butter and sugar until light and add the egg yolk. Then add cassia and currants and gradually add in the flour. Knead well and roll out on a floured board. Cut into circles and place on greased tins.

Bake in a cool oven at 275°F (140°C) Gas Mark 1 for about 10 minutes until pale brown. Let the biscuits cool for a couple of minutes before removing to a wire rack, when quite cold put in an air-tight tin. These biscuits are traditionally eaten at Easter-time.

These craftsmen set new fashions in furniture by using far more walnut and beechwood, and made lighter furniture with the use of caning. They were very skilful in their use of wood and at furniture decoration using veneer, cross-banding and marquetry in walnut.

Towards the end of the century, in reaction from Commonwealth austerity, there was a desire for more opulence and also for more comfort. We can read in Pepys' Diary how he furnished his dining room with heavy green curtains and had gilded leather chairs, but in 20 or 30 years fashion changed considerably, and we can see at Blickling Hall in Norfolk a magnificent set of chairs which are high-back and made of walnut. People were wanting to be more comfortable and so by the end of the century large upholstered chairs were made much as we know them today. There is a good example in Bristol Museum; it has a wooden frame and has a carved rail of stained beechwood at the bottom in front and it has arms and a high back with wings. All of it is well padded and upholstered and completely covered in wool and silk needlework. Such a chair is really comfortable and warm.

The Huguenots also brought to England some new objects for domestic use such as the soup tureen and the sauceboat and the idea of having a handle on a candlestick.

Chamber candlestick

The Countesse of RUTLANDS Receipt of making the rare Banbury Cake, which was so much praised at her daughters (the Right Honorable Lady Chaworths) Wedding.

Imprimis.

Take a peck of fine flower, and halfe an Ounce of large Mace, half an ounce of Nutmeggs, and halfe an ounce of Synamon, your Synamon and Nutmegs must be sifted through a searce, two pounds of butter, halfe a score of Eggs, put out four of the whites of them, somthing above a pint of good Ale yest, beat your Eggs very well and strain them with your yest, and a little warm water into your flower, and stirr them together, then put your butter cold in little Lumps: The water you knead withall must be scalding hot, if you will make it good past, the which having done, lay the past to rise in a warme Cloth a quarter of an hour, or thereabouts; Then put in ten pounds of currants, and a little Musk and Amber-greece dissolved in Rosewater, your currants must be made very dry or else they will make your Cake heavy, strew as much Sugar finely beaten amongst the Currants, as you shall think the Water hath taken away the sweetness from them, break your past into little peices, into a kimnell or such like thing, and lay a Layer of past broken into little peices, and a Layer of Currants, untill your Currants are all put in, mingle the past, and the Currants very well, but take heed of breaking the Currants, you must take out a peice of past after it hath risen in a warm cloath before you put in the currants to cover the top and the bottom you must role the cover something thin and the Bottom likewise, and wet it with Rosewater and close them at the bottom of the side or the middle which you like best, prick the top and the sides with a small long Pin, when your Cake is ready to go into the Oven, cut it in the midst of the side round about with a Knife an inch deep, if your Cake be of a peck of Meale it must stand two hours in the Oven, your Oven must be as hot as for Manchet.

Petworth House was built almost entirely between 1688 and 1696 by Charles Seymour, the 6th Duke of Somerset. He commissioned Grinling Gibbons to adorn the house and he created limewood carvings of dead game, fruit, flowers and musical instruments that are artistic triumphs; they positively riot over the wall surfaces of the Carved Room, they have such vitality.

Gibbons was the most gifted wood carver ever to have worked in England, using softwoods like pear and lime he created life-size and life-like festoons and garlands of fruit and flowers. John Evelyn in his diary noted on 30 July 1682:

We went often to visit our good neighbour Mr Bohune, whose whole house is a Cabinet of all elegancies, an excellent Pendule Clock inclosed in the curious flower work of Mr Gibbons in the midst of the Vestibule is very remarkable. Above all his Lady's Cabinet, adorned on the fret, ceiling and chimny piece with Mr Gibbon's best carving.

There is an extraordinary account in John Evelyn's diary of the way in which Grinling Gibbons' talents were discovered. The diarist was walking near his home in the country when he saw a young man in a poor cottage carving a picture frame. He

Wedding or Christmas Cake

1 lb/450 g flour
1 teaspoon mixed spice
1 lb/450 g sultanas
1 lb/450 g currants
1/2 lb/225 g raisins
1/2 lb/225 g mixed peel
1/2 lb/225 g glacé cherries
1/2 lb/225 g blanched almonds
12 oz/350 g butter
12 oz/350 g castor sugar
8 eggs
1 orange and 1 lemon
1 tablespoon gravy browning
1 glass of brandy

Grate rind of lemon and orange and squeeze out the juice. Prepare a 10 inch cake tin.

Mix the fruit with the flour and spice. Beat the butter and sugar until creamy and then beat in the eggs one at a time. Stir in the fruit, then the rind and juice of the lemon and orange, then browning and brandy. Put in the tin and shake down well to get a flat surface. Bake in a cool oven at 320°F (170°C) Gas Mark 3 for 1 1/2 hours and then reduce heat to 275°F (140°C) Gas Mark 1 for a further 1 1/2 hours. Test.

Cool on a rack. The next day prick with a fine skewer and pour more brandy into the holes. Wrap cake in greaseproof paper and keep in an airtight tin for a month or two as it improves with keeping. Ice with almond paste and royal icing with lemon juice in it.

asked if he might come in and says: "I saw him about such work, as for the curiosity of handling, drawing and studious exactness, I never in my life had seen in all my travels". Evelyn took him and the picture up to London to show the King and Queen and other members of the Court, and very quickly Grinling Gibbons was given commissions and became established.

It is an odd fact that our first realistic botanic art was not in the form of botanical drawings, but of exquisite wood carvings. A little later Pine made drawings and engravings of plants, their flowers, leaves and seeds, but Gibbons had already studied in minute detail the construction of each flower before he carved it.

Limewood cravat by Grinling Gibbons

137

PRESERVES

To make a Quiddony of all kindes of Plums

Take your Apple water and boyl the plums in it till it be red as Claret Wine and when you have made it strong of the Plums, put to every pinte half a pound of Sugar, and so boyl it till a drop of it hang on the back of a spoon like a quaking gelly. If you will have it of an Amber colour, then boyl it with a quick fire, that is all the difference of the colouring of it.

Harvest time was one of intense activity with everyone on the farm working in a body and at the highest pitch from dawn to dusk to gather in the crop. Crowds of workers and children would work together and go from field to field reaping, binding and carrying. When all was safely gathered into the barns there was much rejoicing and feasting as a good harvest meant there was enough to last through the coming winter and early summer. If the harvest was poor then great economy had to be exercised, and even then there would be a state of semi-starvation by the Spring.

"Piers Plowman" tells of the struggle to exist during the last few months before the next harvest:

> *I have no penny, quoth Piers, pullets for to buy,*
> *Neither goose nor griskin; but two green cheeses,*
> *A few curds and cream, and a cake of oats,*
> *And bread for my bairns of beans and peases,*
> *And yet I say, by my soul, I have no salt bacon;*
> *Not a cockney, by Christ, collops to make.*
> *But I have leek-plants, parsley and shallots,*
> *Onions and pot herbs and cherries, half red....*
> *By this livelihood we must live till Lammas-time,*
> *And by that I hope to have harvest in my croft,*
> *Then may I dight my dinner as me dearly liketh.*

We can read of a farmer's wife in the eighteenth century who, with her maids, spent 2 days cooking and baking to get ready enough food for the Harvest home. They roasted fowls, boiled hams and made many pasties; also tarts and puddings with sweet plums, currants, sugar and cinnamon. The labourers all arrived at 7 o'clock and one of them brought his fiddle. The farmer cut up the fowls and hams and gave each person "a goodlie lot, and they did fall to and ett it up right speedlie". Then they ate the "tartes and pudden hartlie". They drank cider and the fiddler played and one or two sang songs and then they all sang together and the cider kept flowing.

Plum Chutney

3 lb/1.35 kg plums
4 lb/1.825 kg apples
3 lb/1.35 kg brown sugar
1 lb/450 g tomatoes
1 lb/450 g onions
1 pint malt vinegar
1 lb/450 g raisins
2 cloves garlic
1 heaped teaspoon ginger
1 heaped teaspoon mixed spice
Chillies (minced, if liked)

Stone plums and slice tomatoes, put in a preserving pan with the vinegar and bring to the boil slowly.
Mince cored apples, peeled onions and add to the pan.
Add sugar, garlic and spices and raisins. Stir well to melt sugar and boil slowly for about an hour then test for set. Pot and seal.

These Harvest homes, or feasts, usually took place in a large barn and the tradition still survives in some places although with mechanization there are far fewer people working on farms and gathering in the harvest. The feeling of working as a community has largely disappeared. Some large farms in East Anglia still celebrate the end of the harvest with a feast known as a horkie.

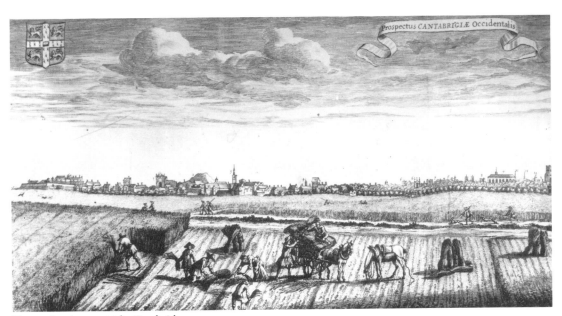

Harvesting just outside Cambridge

> ## To make Quiddony of Pippins of Ruby or an Amber colour
>
> *Take Pippins and cut them in quarters, and pare them and boyl them with as much fair water as will cover them, till they be tender, and sunk into the water, then strain all the liquor from the pulp, then take a pinte of that liquor, and half a pound of Sugar, and boyl it till it be like a quaking gelly, on the back of a spoon, so then pour it on your moulds, being taken out of fair water; then being cold turn them on a wet trencher, and so slide them into the boxes, and if you will have it ruby colour, then boyl it leisurely close covered, till it be as red as Claret wine so may you conceive, the difference is in the boyling of it, remember to boyle your Quinces in Apple water as you doe your plums.*

A bumper crop of apples was a cause for much rejoicing as well as much hard work. Every apple was kept for food for the winter. The windfalls could be made into apple solid and kept for up to a year. This method was widely used. A friend who was given it when she came to lunch one day said she had not had it since she was a child in Czechoslovakia in the 1930s.

Palladius writes about storing apples:

> *Lay them dark as wind may not come near,*
>
> *And do fair straw upon them, fleyke them under.*

This is still good for hand-picked apples – put them on slatted wooden shelves in a windproof shed and put a little straw over them. See that they do not touch each other so that if one goes bad it does not infect its neighbour.

Apples were also dried whole. They were peeled and cored and threaded on strings and hung up in the kitchen ceiling to dry. An apple corer was made from the shank bone of sheep, cut across at a slant and filed into shape. This was inserted into the centre of the apple, twisted round and pulled out bringing the core with it. It was most effective and did not rust, bend or discolour the apple.

Dried apples were used a good deal in the cooking of pork and bacon, either with it in a stew, or put in a stoneware jar with water, sealed tight and lowered into the stewpot beside the meat. They could also be used, not soaked, but chopped up very small with currants, raisins or other dried fruit for a fruit cake; this was done during the last war when dried fruit was so scarce.

By long tradition small eating apples were made into toffee apples and sold at fairs, particularly St. Bartholomew's fair for his saint's day is on 24 August. Before the importation of plantation sugar these would have been dipped into a toffee of honey and beeswax. Now they can be made with a coating of iridescent gold that crackles.

Melt 1/4 lb butter, and 1/2 lb treacle, 1 lb brown sugar and 1 tablespoon of vinegar. Boil for 20 minutes. Put sticks into the core of rosy little apples and dip quickly into the toffee – put on buttered plates. They are very good for Halloween parties.

Apple Solid

6 lb/3 kg apples
4 lb/2 kg sugar
2 pints water
12 cloves
1 cinnamon stick

Peel and core the apples and slice them into a preserving pan; add water. Put cloves and cinnamon into a muslin bag, tie tightly on to the handle of the pan so that it dangles into the apples. Bring to the boil and when soft add the sugar. Boil for about an hour and then test for set by putting a little on a plate and see if it goes skinny on top when cold. It should be golden brown and very thick indeed and should be stirred all the time at the end of cooking so that it does not stick to the pan. It is so thick that it splutters so either use a very long handled spoon or wear rubber gloves during these last few minutes.

Put into pudding basins, 4 large or 6 small ones, cover with greaseproof paper tightly and keep in a dry place. They will keep for a year.

Serve with cream or ice-cream.

This is a good way of using windfall cooking apples and having something in the store cupboard for unexpected guests.

St Bartholomew's Fair at Smithfield

PRESERVES

To pickle Broom Buds

Take your Budds before they be yellow on the top, make a Brine of Vinegar and Salt, which you must do only by shaking it together till the Salt be melted, then put in your Budds and keep stirred on in a day till they be sunk with in the Vinegar, be sure to keep close covered.

"To pickle Lila, an Indian pickle" was a recipe that first came to England in 1694 but what Lila was, or whether Lila was the cook history does not relate. Anyhow, home-made piccalilli is usually much nicer than bought piccalilli.

Pickling was a good way of preserving fruit, vegetables and even nuts for the winter and provided a variety of flavours to go with bread and cheese, and with the salt meat. In an eighteenth-century book there is a description of a farmer's wife getting ready the vinegar for pickling. One day in the middle of June her husband came in to say the: "cyder be sharp and sower". This cider must have been made the previous autumn. So the farmer's wife and her servant got out some vats and filled them with the sour cider and put them in the hot sun. Into each vat they put 2 handfuls of salt and stirred it well and left it for a few days; then they stirred it again and left it for a week. It was then brought into the kitchen and put in the chimney corner for another week. After this they strained it clear and put it in a cask ready to use for pickling. So cider unfit for drinking any longer was turned to good use as vinegar.

Some of the old recipes mention Verjuice, and this was much used in the place of vinegar in ordinary cooking. It was the acid juice of unripe grapes or crab apples which had been crushed with beetles (wooden mallets) and strained. It was very sharp to taste but gave a piquancy to dishes. Some people used it during the war when lemons were unattainable.

Pickled walnuts are delicious if you, or a friend, have a walnut tree. The nuts need to be picked early before the shells have hardened inside their green overcoats. If a darning needle goes through them easily then all is well, but beware of the juice which stains most horribly. Prick the nuts all over with a needle and put them into a brine made up of 3 oz of salt to each pint of water. After 3 days change the brine and leave for a week. Then take out and rinse the nuts under running cold water; spread them out on a tray to dry in the sun. Put 2 oz peppercorns, 1 oz allspice, 8 cloves and a bayleaf in a muslin bag and boil them in 2 pints of vinegar for 10 minutes and leave to cool a little. Put the nuts into jars and pour over the vinegar. Keep for 2 months before eating – they are good with cold turkey.

Piccalilli

3 lb/1.35 kg mixed vegetables (courgettes, tomatoes, runner beans, onions, cauliflower, red cabbage, cucumber, etc.)

salt

3 oz/75 g sugar

1 pint/575 ml white vinegar

1 teaspoon turmeric

1 dessertspoon dry mustard

1 dessertspoon ground ginger

1 tablespoon cornflour

Cut all the vegetables into small pieces and put on a large dish and sprinkle with salt; put another plate on top and weight it down. Leave overnight and the next day rinse the vegetables and drain very well.

Put vinegar, spices and sugar into a large pan and heat gently stirring with a wooden spoon until the sugar is melted.

Add the vegetables and simmer for 10 minutes. Blend the cornflour with a spoonful of vinegar and stir into the vegetables; bring to the boil for a few minutes so as to thicken. Pour into warm pots and seal.

Making cider

To make clear Cakes of Plums

Take plums of any sorts, Respisses are the best, put them into a stone Jugge into a pot of seething water, and when they are dissolved strain them together through a fair cloth, and take to a pinte of that a pound of Sugar, put to as much colour as will melt it, and boyl to a Candy heighth; boyl the liquor likewise in another Posnet, then put them seething hot together, and so boyl a little while stirring them together, then put them into glasses, and set them in an Oven or Stove in a drying heat, let them stand fo two or three weeks, and never be cold, removing them from one warm place to another, they will turn in a week; beware you set them not too hot, for they will be tough: so every day turn them till they be dry; they will be very clear.

Hedgerows and woodlands provided some food for the farm-workers and blackberries, rose-hips and rowan berries could be picked, often by the children, and either eaten at once or made into conserve or jelly. There is a school log-book from the last century which records that the children were given some afternoons off school so that they could go blackberrying.

Elder was much used for the buds were pickled and used instead of capers and were much cheaper for the real capers were imported in barrels from the Mediterranean countries. Elder flowers were beaten into the dough of cakes or made into fritters, boiled in gruel as a drink for the fever, distilled to flavour vinegar, or put into a salad. They can be added to gooseberries being stewed to make gooseberry fool and then taken out before the gooseberries are made into purée; they add a pleasant and unusual flavour. Elderberries collected in autumn made very good syrups and cordials and Cobbett writing nearly 2 centuries later, says that on a cold winter night, "that cup of mulled elder wine served with nutmeg and sippets of toast is a thing to be run for".

Crocus sativus, or saffron

Blackberry Cheese

6 to 10 lb of blackberries

sugar

Put the fruit in a large pan and add enough water to nearly cover it. Simmer gently to a pulp. Take the pulp and sieve it through a nylon sieve (not a metal one); weigh the pulp. Add equal weight of sugar to pulp and heat and stir until the sugar has dissolved. Boil for about an hour until it has reached a semi-solid consistency.

Put into warm jars and seal. Straight-sided jars are needed so that the cheese comes out easily in a roll and can be cut in slices, or else use small pudding basins, or old slop basins from Victorian tea sets which are sometimes pretty shapes. The cheese will keep for months. Serve with cream.

Alternatively damsons may be used to make a cheese.

Saffron, much grown at Saffron Walden, held pride of place for centuries – this is the blossom of the crocus satives, and was very highly valued as a perfume, flavouring, colouring and medicine. It was thought to be a preventative for the Plague. Cooks loved the colour it gave to perhaps otherwise rather dreary looking dishes such as broths, soups, hashes and stews, or rather grey bread, pastry and puddings if the flour was not very white. Certainly it must have put a cheering complexion on many a meal.

One person experimented with the sunflower and says: "Ere it comes to expand and shows its golden face, being dressed as an artichook, it is eaten as a daintie". He also tried the seeds but unsuccessfully, "I once made macaroons with the ripe blanched seeds but the turpentine so domineered over all that it did not answer expectation". Artichokes were considered, "a daintie dish boyled with the broth of fat flesh, but it engendereth melancholy".

Spicy clove carnations were made into a syrup that was used as a sauce for puddings. These flowers were commonly called sops-in-wine for there was a custom of throwing some of them into casks of wine "to give a pleasant taste and gallant colour".

I *Rubus.*
The Bramble Buſh.

Blackberries

PRESERVES

To make Orange Marmalet.

Take Oranges, pare them as thin as you can, boyl them in four several waters, let them be very soft before you take them out, then take two quarts of Spring water, put thereto twenty Pippins pared, quartered and coared, let them boyl till all the virtue be out; take heed they doe not lose the colour; then strain them, put to every pinte of water a pound of Sugar, boyl it almost to a Candie heighth, then take out all the meat out of the Oranges, slice the Pill in long slits as thin as you can, then put in your pill with the juyce of two Limons and one half Orange, then boyl it to a Candy.

There is a legend about the naming of marmalade. In 1548 Mary, Queen of Scots, as a small girl aged 5 fled from Scotland to France, to the protection of the French Court. After a terrible and exhausting journey she arrived home-sick and ill. Her lady-in-waiting made a conserve of oranges to comfort her and so "Marie malade" became marmalade.

A century later it appears in Queen Henrietta Maria's cookery book and so on down the centuries. Now we use Seville oranges which are ripe in January; they are very bitter, contain a lot of pectin and so make good marmalade that sets into a firm jelly.

These oranges will also survive freezing and so a few may be kept in the freezer to flavour other dishes. The juice is particularly good for adding to chocolate desserts or icings; it gives them a tangy taste and dispels any cloyingness of the chocolate.

Oranges originally came from Persia and in Arabic were called naranj. They came west and probably came into Spain with the Moors. They were much liked in the seventeenth century and appear in many meat and poultry recipes though they were still something of a luxury. Orange and lemon trees were grown "in potts of earth and so moved about from place to place and into the aire sometymes" in some of the Oxford and Cambridge Colleges.

They were sold in the streets of London and eaten in theatres. Nell Gwynne lived precariously as an orange girl before going on the boards at Drury Lane theatre. She quickly established herself as a comedienne, especially in "breeches parts", and was known as "Pretty, witty Nellie". She became Charles II's mistress and had at least one son by him, Charles Beauclerk, Duke of St. Albans.

There is a list of plate at Gilling in Yorkshire which mentions a silver "cullander for orringes" weighing 5 oz which presumably was for straining the juice of oranges. In one of the recipes in the original book the writer bids the cook to "be sure none of your orange kernells be amongst your pie-meat", and so a "cullander for orringes" would be useful.

Seville Orange Marmalade

3 lb/1.4 kg seville oranges
2 lemons
5 pints/2.8 L water
6 lb/2.7 kg sugar
1 teaspoon black treacle

Cut oranges and lemons in half and squeeze the juice and pips into a basin. Cut the peel into thin strips and put in a large preserving pan with the water.

Strain the juice from the basin into the preserving pan and then put the pips into a muslin bag, tie tightly at the neck and then tie it onto the handle of the pan letting the bag dangle into the water. Leave all overnight to soak as this will soften the peel.

Next day bring to the boil and lift out the bag of pips squeezing it between two spoons, discard. Add the warmed sugar and boil until it reaches setting point. Let it cool a little and remove any scum. Stir it well to distribute the peel and then add the treacle to give a richer colour. Pot and seal.

Beadwork basket

To make Artificial Fruits

Take a mould made of Alabaster, three yelks, and tye two pieces together, and lay them in water an hour, and take as much Sugar as will fill up your mould, and boyl it to a Manus Christi, then pour it into your mould suddenly, and clap on the lid, round it about with your hand, and it will be whole and hollow, then colour it with what colour you please, half red, or half yellow, and you may yellow it with a little Saffron steept in water.

Probably the most eccentric traveller in the early seventeenth century was Thomas Coryate, a son of a Somerset rector, who was educated at Oxford. He then became "a priveledged buffoon" in the household of Prince Henry. Fuller tells us he had an extraordinary memory and an "admirable fluency in the Greek tongue". He lived by his wits at Court until his father died in 1608 and then he set off on his travels probably having inherited a little money. He sailed from Dover on 14 May, and walked or got lifts in carts to Paris, Lyons, crossed the Mont Cenis and visited Turin, Milan and Padua before arriving in Venice on 24 June. He wrote: "I saw Venice, which yielded the most glorious and heavenly show upon the water that ever any mortal eye beheld, such a show as did ravish me with delight and admiration". Here he settled down for 6 weeks.

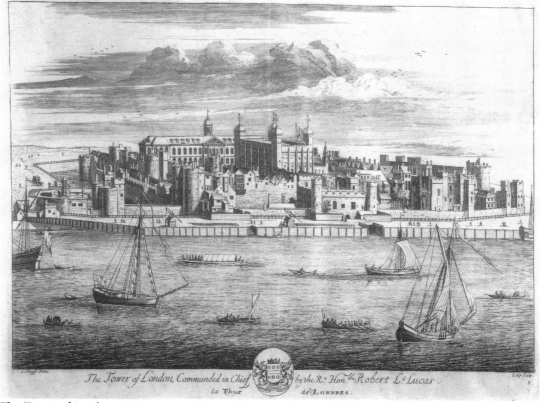

The Tower of London (Bodleian, Douce Prints a 24, plate 5)

Tangerine Fudge

2 oz/50 g butter
1/4 pint/150 ml milk
1 lb/450 g light brown sugar
pinch of salt
skins of 2 or 3 tangerines

Melt butter and milk and add sugar and salt. Bring slowly to the boil and continue to boil for about 7 minutes.

Cut tangerine skins into fine shreds and add to the mixture. Butter a dish. Test for set by dropping a little of the mixture into a cup of cold water. When it is ready it will form a firm ball in the water. Take off the heat and leave to cool for 5 minutes, and then beat until much cooler and it goes thick, heavy and granulated. Quickly pour into the buttered dish. Cut into squares before it is quite cold

Coryate was fascinated by the abundance of fruit and vegetables to be had in spite of the Venetians having "neither meadows, nor pastures, nor arable land near their city". He found "the most delectable dish for a Sommer fruit of all Christendom was the Muske Melons". But he found them "Sweet-sowre, sweet in the palate, but sowre in the stomache if not soberly eaten". Obviously too much wine had been taken. He seems to have missed coming through the Brenta district on the mainland which is flat and very fertile with innumerable little waterways. It was a very flourishing district in his day, and for some 60 years previously architects like Palladio had been building large airy villas for the wealthiest Venetians so that they could spend the hottest summer months amidst gardens, orchards and vineyards. Plenty of vegetables, fruit and Muske Melons must have been brought into Venice by boat each day.

Arriving back in London via Switzerland and Germany he tried to publish his journal but no publisher would take the risk so Coryate asked all his Court friends to write commendatory verses on himself, his travels and his journal. This they did, all trying to outdo each other, and it was published as *Coryate's Crudities, Hastily Gobbled Up In Five Months' Travels*. It was a great success and was the first continental handbook for travel.

Coryate started on his travels again visiting Constantinople, Greece, Cairo and the Holy Land before joining a caravan to go through Mesopotamia and Persia to Candabar and Lahore. At Agara he was welcomed by English merchants who had a "factory" but he did not mention what was traded. He wrote letters home to his friends, some of which were published with an amusing illustration of Coryate riding on an elephant. He lived a year in India before dying at the age of 40 of "the flux".

To candie Pippins, Pears, Apricocks, or Plums

Take any of these fruits being pared, and strew upon them as you doe flowre upon frying fish; then lay them on a board in a pewter dish; so put them into an Oven as hot as for Manchet; as the liquor comes from them pour forth, turne them, and strew more Sugar on them, and sprinkle Rose-water on them, thus turning and Sugaring of them three or four times, till they be almost dry, then lay them on a lettice Wyer, or on the botom of a Sive in a warm Oven, after the bread is drawn out, till they be full dry; so you may keep them all the year.

Lady in a Stillroom (Bodleian, Vet.A4 e 713. Frontispiece)

The kitchen and the stillroom, which was also a dispensary and surgery, were closely linked centuries ago. The lady of the house or the farmer's wife became very knowledgeable not only about food and how to preserve it, but also about medicines and how to treat wounds from accidents, adder bites, wasp stings and such like. She would be the person to whom her husband's employees would turn to in an emergency as doctors were not often near at hand.

Each year at the right season she would make up a supply of medicines and ointments so that they would be there ready when the cook was scalded, or the scullery maid cut herself, or a farm boy fell off a waggon, or a labourer ruptured himself lifting a heavy barrel. She had to think ahead and plan carefully for most of her medicines were made from herbs and plants. Her herb garden had to be well stocked and tended and old plants renewed when necessary. They had to be picked and used, or stored, when they were in bud, or in flower each according to the recipe.

Apple and Ginger Chutney

2^1/$_2$ lb/1.125 g apples

3 onions

1 lb/450 g brown sugar

^{1}/$_2$ lb/225 g sultanas

^{1}/$_2$ teaspoon salt

1^1/$_2$ pints/875 ml vinegar

2 oz/50 g mustard seed

2 oz/50 g crystallized ginger (more if liked)

1 dessertspoon of pickling spice

Peel and chop the apples and slice the onions and cook in the vinegar till soft. Put the spice in a muslin bag and hang in the pan. Add sugar, sultanas and salt and continue to cook until fairly solid.

Chop up ginger into little bits. Take the chutney off the heat and add the ginger and mustard seed, stir well..

Pour into warm pots and seal.

So Lady Goring recommended that Hoggs' fat clarified and beaten into egg white till it became an ointment, should be kept ready to put on burns and scalds, "annoynting the sore twice a day".

Lady Mildmaye's remedy for a cough was to:

take liquorish sliced, anniseed, figs, raisons of the sun and hysop tops each a little handful, and a great handful of coltsfoot and boil in a gallon of water till it is half consumed. Then strain it and stir in four good spoonfuls of honey, and take it warm in the morning, at four in the afternoon and when you go to bed.

We can see that both these recipes would bring relief to the patient.

Not only was the herb garden used, but the hedgerows and woods as well, and the old cookery book recommends collecting:

Southernwood, wormwood, bugle, mugwort, sanicle, plantain, dandilion, cinquefoil, ribwort, wood betany, herb bennet, hawthorne buds, agrimony, oak leaves and buds, angelica, mints, scabious, strawberry leaves, violet leaves and comfrey in May, each twenty handfuls, and dry them, turn them often that they may not become musty, then put them up severally in Canvas bags.

These would hang in the Stillroom ready for use.

All "worts" like St. John's wort, were good plants and could be used, and all "banes" like fleabane were bad plants and were not to be used.

To make Paste of Apricocks

Take your Apricocks, and pare them, and stone them, then boyl them tender betwixt two dishes on a Chafing Dish of coals, then being cold lay it forth on a white sheet of paper, then take as much Sugar as it doth weigh, and boyl it to a candy heighth, with as much Rose-water and fair water as will melt the Sugar; then put the pulp into the hot Sugar, and so let it boyl till it be as thick as for Marmalet, now and then stirring of it; then fashion it upon a Pye plate like to half Apricocks and the next day close the half Apricocks, to the other, and when they are dry they will be as clear as Amber, and eat much better than Apricocks it self.

A fair, or good complexion was greatly prized in the days when small-pox was rife and so many people were pock-marked. For small-pox left little scars and dents in the skin if you survived the disease.

The King had it lightly fairly soon after his marriage but fortunately the Queen did not catch it from him. However, Princess Anne died of it at the age of 3, and Princess Mary and Prince Henry both died of it when grown-up, so even when people were living in good conditions it was a killer.

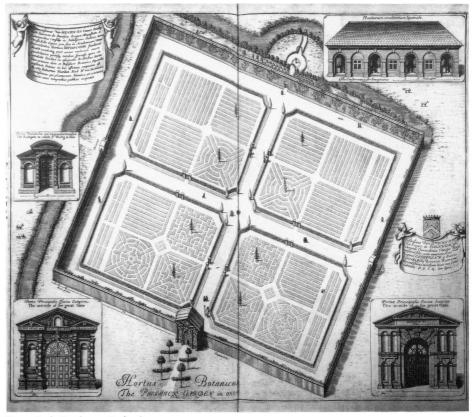

Botanical Gardens, Oxford (Bodleian, Arch.Antiq A11.13 (12), plate 12)

Cranberry and Walnut Chutney

4 large oranges
8 oz/225 g brown sugar
1 lb/450 g cranberries
6 oz/175 g walnuts
2 cinnamon sticks
6 cloves
good pinch of nutmeg

Put cloves and cinnamon in a muslin bag to hang in the pan. Grate rind off oranges and squeeze the juice and put in the pan. Add sugar and dissolve over a low heat stirring all the time. Add the cranberries and boil for about 5 minutes until they are cooked and soft. Chop the walnuts, not too small, and stir them in.

Pot in warm pots and seal.

There is a recipe in the old book for an "Oyntment for the Pocks when they begin to change at top and to prevent holes". It tells you to clarify bacon fat and then mix it with Red Rose Water. Put it in a Gallypot and "when you will use it, melt it, and with a feather anoynt the Face day and night, once in a quarter of an hour, till the scabs to clean off, and afterwards as long as there remaineth any scurfe". This would presumably ease the itching of the scabs and remind the patient not to scratch.

There are many remedies for pimples and suggestions as to how to have a fair complexion for example: "An approved Medicine to beautifie the Face, or to take away Pimples or Heat in the Face":

Take a fair earthen Pipkin, and put into it a pottle of clean running water, and an ounce of white Mercury beaten to white powder, then set it on the fire, and let it boil until one half be consumed, and keep it close covered saving when you stir it, then take the whites of six new laid egs beaten half an hour or more, and put it into the liquor, after it is taken from the fire, you must put in also the juice of Lemons being very good, and half a pint of new Milk, and a quarter of a pound of bitter Almonds blanched and beaten with half a pint of Damask Rose-water; strain all these together through a strainer, and let it stand three weeks before you use it, and I will warrant you fair.

Now we know that it is dangerous to use mercury like this, so it would have been safer to "take fresh bean blossoms and distill them in a Limback and with the water wash your face". For pimples you could try taking "the Liverwort that groweth in the well, stamp it and strain it, and put the juice into cream and so anoynt your face as long as you will and it will help you". Or if your problem was a shiny nose you could try taking "12 oz of Gourd seed, crackle them and take out the kernels, peel off the skin, and blanch 6 oz of bitter almonds and make an oyle of them, and anoynt the place grieved therewith; use it often".

It is small wonder that this little book was so popular that it ran into 10 editions.

To make good Vinegar

Take one strike of Malt, and one of Rye, ground and mash them together, and take if they be good, three pound of Hops if not four pound; make two Hogs heads of the best of that Malt and Rye, then lay the Hogsheads where the sunne may have power over them, and when it is ready to Tun, fill your hogsheads where they lye, then let them purge cleer and cover them with two slate stones, and within a week after when you bake, take two cheat loaves hot out of the Oven, and put into each hogshead a loafe, you must use this foure times, you must brew this in Aprill, and let it stand till June, then draw them clearer, then wash the hogsheads cleane, and put the Beer in again, if you will have it Rose-vinegar, you must put in a strike and a half of Roses, if Elder-vinegar a peck of the flowres, if you will have it white, put nothing in it after it is drawn, and so let it stand till Michaelmas, if you will have it coloured red, take four gallons of strong Ale as you can get, and Elder-berries picked a few full clear, and put them in your pan with the Ale, set them over the fire till you guesse that a pottle is wasted, then take it off the fire, and let it stand till it be stone cold, and the next day strain it into the Hogshead, then lay them in a Cellar or Buttery, which you please.

The more well-off ladies spent hours doing needlework with which to decorate their houses, sets of chair covers or cushion covers embroidered with wool in tent stitch and perhaps edged with silver bobbin lace. Purses, or little sweet bags for sweet-smelling herbs were woven in silks and metallic threads. Little caps were finely embroidered, and towards the end of the century so were stomachers. These were made of linen and sewn with coloured silks in satin stitch and metal threads in couched and laid work. They were usually bound round the edge in silk ribbon.

All household linen, of course, had to be hemmed by hand and if the pillow cases were to be edged with lace then this had to be made and whipped on by hand too.

Bed curtains were made and often elaborately embroidered or decorated with braid or silver or gold lace all to be sewn on with tiny stitches. Bed coverlets could be very grand and impressive as friends were often entertained in bedchambers, and there is a nice picture of one young lady in bed soon after her confinement holding court to her women friends and having the new baby admired. At the beginning of the century the great bed in the Pearl Bedchamber at Hardwick Hall had hangings of black velvet embroidered with gold and silver thread and studded with pearls. The valances were trimmed with black, gold and silver fringe. The counterpane was richly worked with pearls and coiled silver wire. By the end of the century taste had changed and become lighter and more delicate. There is a bed coverlet of cream satin embroidered with coloured silks and metal threads in satin stitch, long and short stitch, French knots and couching. The design is mostly of flowers and some early examples of chinoiserie motifs.

Stump work was all the fashion either as pictures or in the form of caskets. These were miniature chests-of-drawers, about 1 or 1½ foot high, made of wood and covered with embroidered silk. They usually showed Biblical or classical scenes.

Green Tomato Chutney

8 lb/3.65 kg green tomatoes

3 large onions

1 pint/575 ml malt vinegar

1¹/₂ pints/875 ml water

1 lb/450 g sultanas

2 lb/900 g brown sugar

1 tablespoon of each of the following: ginger,
mustard, cloves, allspice and cinnamon.

salt

Cut the tomatoes and onions in slices and put in layers with the salt sprinkled over them; leave overnight and then drain very well.

Put all the ingredients in a large pan except the sugar and boil until soft; add the sugar and boil till pulpy and thick. Pour into warm jars and seal.

Another favourite subject was Charles II hiding in an oak tree. The pictures were worked in silks with a satin stitch and chain stitch background, and the figures were padded so as to stand out and be almost 3-dimensional and had real hair. The leaves and acorns of the tree were free standing made of silver wire. The King's armour would be very realistically made of tiny silver sequins. The whole would be exquisitely made and have great charm, but looks somewhat bizarre to us today as scale, proportion and perspective were not taken into consideration.

Stumpwork

Mary Thurston's counterpane

To make Sirup of Rasberries

Take nine quarts of Rasberries, clean pickt and gathered in a dry day, and put to them four quarts of good Sack, into an earthen pot, then paste it up very close, and set in a seller for ten daies, then distil it in a glasse or Rose Still, then take more Sack and put in Rasberries to it, then when it hath taken out all the colour of the Raspis, strain it out, and put in some fine Sugar to your taste, and set it on the fire, keeping it continually stirring till the scum doe rise, then take it off the fire, let it not boyle, skim it very clean, and when it is cold put it to your distilled Raspis; but colour it no more then to make it a pale Claret Wine. This put into bottles or glasses stopt very close.

The daughters in yeomen's families were taught to sew and often to spin and weave as well, as most country women made clothes and household linen for their own households, or even to sell at local markets. Girls were taught to sew from an early age as we can tell from contemporary samplers, and how to mend and patch as well, as clothes and bed linen became worn.

Quilted bodice

Garden Delight

5 or 6 lb/3 kg (approximately) fresh fruit
bottle of brandy
2 or 3 lbs/1 kg sugar

Take a large stone, or glass jar and at the beginning of the summer put in it about 1 lb/
450 g of strawberries, add 8 oz/225 g sugar and cover with brandy; cover the jar
tightly with plastic film.

Repeat this process at intervals but add other fruit instead of the strawberries;
raspberries, sliced peaches, nectarines, apricots, greengages, and whitecurrants are
good but do not put too many redcurrants, blackcurrants or loganberries as they are
strongly flavoured. Stir gently after each addition and then cover tightly.

Keep till Christmas and then strain. Serve the fruit with cream and meringues, and
serve the fruit brandy as a liqueur.

Fashions in clothes did not change very much if you lived in the country. Dresses
had tightish bodices and long full skirts which were decorated by having a braiding
sewn round the bottom a few inches above the hem line. The long sleeves were set
into large deep armholes and could be rolled up when working. Underneath was
worn a loose, white linen smock. Over the dress would be worn an apron tied
round the waist and often honeycombed, an early form of smocking, to form
gathers, but the shape of the apron was long and narrow.

Deloney speaks of a country girl making hay wearing "a red stamell petticoat and a
broad straw hat". The making of straw hats had become a thriving industry in the
southern part of England. Pepys describes how "at the inn the ladies had pleasure in
putting on some straw hats, which are worn in this country, and did become them
mightily, especially my wife".

In the records of one almshouse it is written that in 1616 the elderly women worn
gowns of blue fustian lined with baize which must have been very warm. Blue was a
poor person's colour in the early days as wool was dyed with locally grown woad.
With the blue gowns the women wore high crowned black hats.

The Puritan influence brought sombre clothes and colours, muted browns and greys
for the women with white collars often drooping to long points in the front.

Both men and women wore stockings kept up with garters tied above the knee.
Stockings were usually of wool and there was quite a cottage industry knitting them.
More exotic ones were made of silk and bright colours were worn by the
fashionable ladies who wished to show an ankle in a flash of colour.

Pattens were worn to keep the wearer high up out of the mud and dirt in the road.
A Swedish visitor to England wrote: "A kind of wooden shoe which stands on a high
iron ring. Into these shoes they thrust their ordinary leather or stuff shoes".

To make Syrrup of Limons or Citrons

Pare off all the rindes, then slice your Limons very thin, and lay a lare of Sugar finely beaten, and a lare of Limons in a silver Bason till you have fitted it, or as much as you mean to make, and so let it stand all night; the next day pour off the liquor that runs from it into a glasse through a Tiffany strainer. Be sure you put Sugar enough to them at the first, and it will keep a yeare good, if it be set up well.

We know that Charlotte de la Tremouille, later Countess of Derby, was shocked by the way the English dressed their babies; she considered it very old fashioned to swaddle infants and then short-coat them so soon. The Royal babies wore long clothes of linen and white satin, followed by three-quarter length robes. The babies, like French babies of the time, always wore white. Both boys and girls wore simple gowns with aprons, collars and little round caps. After the age of 4 the boys wore jackets with lace collars and breeches, and the girls wore square-necked tight bodices and full skirts which were often looped up to give freedom of movement and to display the petticoats underneath. Both sexes grew their hair fairly long and the little princesses had their hair done in curl papers to produce ringlets.

In the summer the Royal Children would be settled in one of the country palaces and would be visited from time to time by their parents. Plague and other infections occurred regularly in London in the summer and so everyone who could left the city.

There were quite a few members of the Court who had young families who were friends for the Princes and Princesses, and the Queen used to include them sometimes in her masques to act and dance. The King and Queen seem to have been interested in children and also caring for them. The King, at his own expense, sent 15,000 London orphans over to a settlement of Roman Catholics in America. This expedition was led by Lord Baltimore and the King named the new settlement Maryland after his wife.

Special furniture was made for children and at the Red Lodge in Bristol there is a high chair made of oak; there is also an oak cradle on rockers and just inside the cradle is a knob to which could be tied a cord which the mother could pull gently and so rock the cradle without getting out of bed herself.

Little girls had dolls and if they were fortunate they were beautiful ones which could be dressed and undressed, though the more ordinary ones were rather like our present day rag dolls, but usually with the legs all in one piece and, of course, long skirts. These were, at that time, known as Poppets and reference is made to them in Arthur Miller's play "The Crucible" about the witch hunt in Salem. The words doll and poppet have changed a little in usage over the centuries and on either side of the Atlantic. In America someone will now say of a pretty little girl "Isn't she a doll" but in England would say "Isn't she a poppet".

Lemon Curd

2 large lemons – rind and juice
3 eggs
8 oz/225 g sugar
2 oz/50 g butter

Heat some water in the bottom of a double saucepan. Put butter and sugar in the saucepan to melt.

Grate the rind off the lemons and extract the juice and put in liquidizer with the eggs and liquidize, or beat the eggs and strain the juice. Put in the saucepan and stir. Continue stirring gently until the mixture thickens and will coat the back of a wooden spoon; this will take 10–15 minutes.

Put into warm jars and fill well up as the curd shrinks a little as it cools and thickens.

Rocking horse

PRESERVES

To preserve Quinces white or red

Take the Quinces, and coat them, and pare them, those that you will have white, put them into a pale of water two or three houres, then take as much Sugar as they weigh, put to it as much water as will make a syrup to cover them, then boyl your syrup a little while, then put your Quinces in, and boyl them as fast as you can, till they be tender and clear, then take them up and boyl the Syrup a little higher by it selfe, and being cold, put them up. And if you will have them red, put them raw into Sugar and boyle them leisurely close covered till they be red, and put them not into cold water.

The Royal nurseries must have been large and busy places with plenty of staff to look after babies arriving so regularly; the first baby died soon after birth in May 1629, but after that they arrived in May 1630, November 1631, October 1633, December 1635, March 1637, January 1639, July 1640 and June 1644.

Boots worn by Charles I as a child   Christening robe

160

Quince Jelly

equal quantities of quinces
and cooking apples
sugar

Peel, core and dice the quinces and apples. Put them in a large pan and cover with water. Stew till soft and then mash and put in a jelly bag to drain over night. Measure the juice and put 1 lb/450 g of sugar to each pint/575 ml of juice. Boil till it sets and is a lovely clear red. It is good on scones, or with meat instead of redcurrant jelly.

We hear of babies being weaned on to Pappe and there is a recipe in The *Queen's Closet Opened* for this:

To Make Pappe:

Take three quarts of new milk, set on the fire in a dry silver dish, or bason, when it begins to boyle skim it, then put thereto a handful of flour and the yelks of three eggs which you must have well mingled together with a ladlefull of cold milk, before you put it to the milk that boyles, and as it boyles stir it all the while till it be enough, and in the boyling season it with a little salt, and a little fine beaten sugar and so keeping it stirred till it be boyled as thick as you desire, then put it forth into another dish and serve it up.

Another nursery recipe is for teething babies as follows:

To Make Childrens Teeth come without Pain, Proved.

Take the head of a hare boyled or roasted, and with the brain thereof mingle honey and butter, and therewith anoynt the childs gum as often as you please.

There is also a recipe for the young and old.

A Purge for Children or Old Men.

Take one spoonful of Spirit of Tartar prepared, with Sugarcandy and Rosewater, put it in a little broth, and give it either of them; it purgeth gently, it comforts the Heart, and expelleth Phlegm and Melancholy.

Hints on midwifery are numerous and sometimes horrific, but here is one on how to start a new-born baby breathing:

The Lady Smiths Remedy to bring a young child when it is born.

Take a little Coventry blew thred, burn it and hold it to the childes nose that the smoak may goe up.

These are a few of the more delicate recipes used in the nursery: there are many unsuitable for a cookery book as they are most unsavoury. The cure seems worse than the ailment. But one daughter was doing well in her pregnacy for her mother writes: "my daughter enjoyeth her health so well that she hath made no use more of the French doctor's arte. I long to hear when she and her great belly doe".

PRESERVES

Samuel Pepys, always curious and ready to try anything, wrote in his journal on 25 September 1660 "I did send for a cup of tea – a china drink of which I never had drunk", but he does not comment on it.

The first printed recipe for making tea is Tea with Eggs, which sounds rather disgusting but would be nourishing and quick to make.

The Jesuits that came from China, 1664, told Mr Waller that there they use it sometimes in this manner. To near a pint of the infusion, take two yolks of new laid eggs, and beat them very well with as much fine sugar as is sufficient for this quantity of liquor; when they are very well incorporated, pour your tea upon the eggs and sugar and stir them very well together. So drink it hot. This is when you come home from attending business abroad, and are very hungry, and yet have not conveniency to eat presently a competent meal. This presently discusseth and satisfieth all rawness and indigence of the stomach, flyeth suddainly over the whole body and into the veins, and strengthneth exceedingly, and preserves one a good while from the necessity of eating. Mr Waller findeth all those effects of it this with eggs. In these parts, he saith, we let the hot water remain too long soaking upon the tea, which makes it extract into itself the earthy parts of the herb. The water is to remain upon it no longer than whiles you can say the Miserere Psalm very leisurely. Then pour it upon the sugar, or sugar and eggs. Thus you have only the spiritual parts of the tea, which is much more active, penetrative and friendly to nature. You may from this regard take a little more of the herb; about 1 dragm of tea will serve for a pint of water which makes three ordinary draughts.

Tea was first imported into Europe by the Dutch East India Company and from Holland into London . The "Mercurius Politicus" published that "Tea is sold at the Sultaness Head Coffee House, in Sweetings Rents by the Royal Exchange".

The English East India Company purchased and presented 2 pounds of tea to Charles II in 1664, but the first order for its importation by the company was not placed until 1668. This first consignment was $143^{1}/_{2}$ lb and was received from Bantam in 1669. It was very expensive and so was kept in specially made little tea caddies with locks and only the mistress of the house had the key. Gradually the price dropped and by the last century it had become our national drink. It is thought that fewer men died in the Crimean war than might have otherwise because the soldiers boiled the water to make their tea.

Pear Pickle

7 lbs/3.2 kg pears (weighed peeled)
4 lbs/1.825 kg sugar
1 stick cinnamon
$^1/_2$ oz/10 g cloves
1 piece ginger root
$^1/_4$ teaspoon allspice
rind of a lemon
3 pints/1$^1/_2$ l vinegar

Crush ginger and put with other spices into a muslin bag. Dissolve sugar in vinegar and add bag of spices.

Cut the fruit into small pieces, add to the vinegar and cook gently until tender.

Remove the pears from the liquid and put into jars, each not more than three-quarters full. Continue to boil the vinegar until it thickens and is considerably reduced, then fill each jar and cover. Store for 2 or 3 months before using and it will have thickened a bit more.

This is a good way of using up hard pears.

The earliest English teapot

PRESERVES

> ## *To preserve Artichoks young, green Walnuts, and Lymons, and the Elicampane roots, or any bitter thing.*
>
> *Take any of these and boyl them tender, and shift them in their boyling six or seven times to take away their bitternesse, out of one hot water into another, then put a quart of Salt unto them, then take them up and dry them with a fair cloth, then put them into as much clarified Sugar as will cover them, then let them boyl a walm or two, and so let them stand soaking in the Sugar till the next morning, then take them up and boyl the Sugar a little higher by it selfe, and when they are cold put them up.*
> *Let your green Walnuts be prickt full of holes with a great pin, and let them not be long in one water, for that will make them look black, being boyled tender stick two or three Cloves in each of them.*
> *Set your Elecampane roots; being clean scraped, and shifted in their boylings a dozen times, then dry them in a fair cloth, and so boyl them as is above written, take halfe so much more than it doth weigh, because it is bitter &c.*

There can have been few more interesting personalities in the Century than Sir Kenelm Digby for he was courtier, naval commander, author, chemist, cook and student of occult lore. He was the son of Sir Everard Digby who suffered death on the scaffold for his complicity in the Gun Powder Plot, but neither this nor his own profession of the Catholic faith seemed to affect his advancement in life.

Kenelm Digby when young

Kenelm Digby at the age of 19 was at the Court of Madrid when Prince Charles and the Duke of Buckingham arrived to court the Infanta, and he joined the Prince's retinue and returned home with him. On his return James I, who had hanged his father, gave him a knighthood and he was granted Letters-of-Marque so he raised a squadron and carried out a very profitable naval expedition in the Mediterranean against the Algerians. Charles I made him Gentleman of the Bedchamber and later he was appointed Chancellor to Queen Henrietta Maria. The Long Parliament clapped him into prison but he was later released, banished into exile and his estates confiscated. He lived at the French Court and returned to England at the Restoration.

Spiced Pears

3 lb/350 kg hard pears
1/2 pint/275 ml cider vinegar
1 1/2 lb/675 g dark brown sugar
1/2 teaspoon each of ginger, cinnamon, cloves

Peel, core and chop up the pears.Put all ingredients in a large casserole and bring to the boil stirring to melt the sugar. Then place the casserole in a cool oven 275°F (140°C) Gas Mark 1 for 3 hours. Test to see that the pears are soft. Leave to get cold and then put into containers and store in the freezer or bottle in Kilner jars. Serve with ice-cream or cream.

On the foundation of the Royal Society Sir Kenelm was appointed one of its first Council and took a very active part in its management for he had always been interested in the sciences. His discourse on the *Vegetation of Plants* was a sound contribution and he gave papers on various topics. He related that when in Spain he had met a young nobleman who was born deaf, but had been taught by his tutor to converse by the movement of the lips (lip reading) but no one in London believed that this could be possible. He dabbled in alchemy and astrology, cooked and brewed. He assembled recipes mostly of drinks and had nearly 50 for making mead and almost as many for metheglin. He lived in a house in Covent Garden which had capacious cellars which were much needed for his brewing and distilling. One recipe reads: "Take sixty gallons of water", so it was all done on a very large scale; one recipe says take 1 gallon of honey to every 3 of water. Most of his wine and all his beer and ale were home-made.

When he died he left his money and possessions to his friends, with whom he had shared Gargantuan meals; he died of a surfeit of good living, overweight, gout and "the stone". His son John edited his collection of recipes and added a final bitter comment to his readers: "Fall to, therefore, and much good may it do thee."

PRESERVES

> ## *To Pickle Oysters*
>
> *Take Oysters and wash them clean in their own Liquor, then let them settle, then strain it, and put your Oysters to it with a little Mace and whole Pepper, as much Salt as you please, and a little Wine Vinegar, then set them over the fire, and let them boyle leasurely till they are pretty tender, be sure to skim them still as the skum riseth; when they are enough, take them out till the Pickle be cold, then put them into any pot that will lye close, they will keep best in Caper barrels, they will keep very well six weeks.*

Sir Kenelm Digby was a close friend of the Queen and was about her household in France for many years. He was appointed her Chancellor in 1645, and she sent him to Rome to raise funds for the royal cause. He had many talks with Pope Innocent X and was given 20,000 crowns from the papal curia.

When in France he expressed the wish to go home to England and live again beneath "smiling English skies", and made several journeys between France and England during the Commonwealth period. His Library, which must have been considerable, he left in Paris, and it was sold after his death for 10,000 crowns. From his writings we have glimpses of the Queen's life at this period. For instance we know what she had for breakfast for he says

The Queen's ordinary Bouillon de saute in the morning was this: A Hen, a handful of parsley, a sprig of Thyme, three of Spear minth, a little balm, half a great onion, a little pepper and salt and a clove, as much water as will cover the Hen and this boiled to less than a pint, for one good porrenger full.

He also writes that "the Queen useth to baste meat with yolks of fresh eggs". This would form a crust over the meat and keep in the juices as it would if you wrapped it in pastry, or kitchen foil. Or perhaps, he means she poured whipped up egg yolks over the meat when it had been carved as a sort of sauce.

Interest in food and cooking seems to have been something he shared with the Queen, and he gives the following recipe which is rather like our present day ginger beer:

Hydromel as I made it for the Queen Mother.

Take eighteen quarts of spring water and a quart of honey. When the water is warm put the honey into it. When it boileth up skim it well, and continue skimming it as long as any scum will rise. Then put in one race of Ginger, slice in thin slices, four cloves and a little sprig of green Rosemary. Let these boil in the Liquor so long till in all it hath been one hour. Then set it to cool till it be blood warm and then put to it a teaspoonful of Ale yeast. When it is worked up, put it into a vessel of fit size and after two or three days bottle it up. You may drink it after six weeks or two months.

This was the hydromel that I gave the Queen which was exceedingly liked by Everybody.

Pickled Eggs

12 fresh eggs (bantam eggs are good)

3 pints/1¹/₂ l malt vinegar

2 oz/50 g pickling spice

Put the vinegar and spices in a large basin and cover with foil. Put the basin in a pan with enough water to come well up the sides. Bring to the boil and then leave to get cold; strain and remove spices.

Hard boil the eggs but stir them a couple of times in the first few minutes so as to centralize the yolks. Plunge into cold water and then take off the shells.

Pack the eggs into glass jars and cover with the spiced vinegar and seal. Keep for at least 3 weeks before eating.

Glass goblet

PRESERVES

To make Paste of Rasberries or English Currants

Take any of the Frails, and boyl them tender on a chasing dish of coals betwixt two dishes and strain them, with the Pap of a roasted Apple, then take as much Sugar as the pulp doth weigh, and boyl to a Candy heighth with as much Rosewater as will melt it, then put the pulp into the hot Sugar, and let it boyl leisurely till you see it as thick as Marmalet, then fashion it on a Pie plate and put it into the Oven on two Billets of wood, that the plate touch not the bottome, and so let them dry leisurely till they be dry.

Pray chuse for me the best sherry sack you can finde in Bristol and send me up forty gallons of itt.

This was a postscript of a letter written in the early 1660s and contemporary with Pepys. Pepys describes in his diary how Thomas Povey kept his cellar "where upon several shelves there stood bottles of all sorts of wine, new and old, with labels pasted upon each bottle, and in that order and plenty as I never saw books in a bookseller's shop". Of course wine would not keep very long in these bottles that were not airtight. Pepys himself records that in 1666 that he has in his cellar:

Two tierces of claret, two quarter cask of canary, and a smaller vessel of sack-a vessel of tent (tinto, a Spanish red wine) another of Malaga, and another of white wine, all in my wine-cellar together – which I believe none of my friends of my name now alive ever had of his own at one time.

As one might expect Pepys was the first Englishman to record the name of the chateau whose claret he had drunk,"ho Bryan" (Haut Brion)

In his late twenties Pepys had obviously indulged too much and found that heavy drinking upset his stomach and gave him bad hangovers. One of his friends finding him with a very bad headache one morning prescribed a drink of chocolate, the first he had ever tasted, but he did not note whether it had helped the hangover.

The recipes in *The Queen's Closet Opened* often suggest cooking with wine: "take the ducks and put them into a Pipkin and put a quart of Claret into it and chestnuts and a pint of great oysters", and in mince pies you put "a quarter of a pint of Sack". There is Master Rudstone's Posset: "take a pint of Sack, a quarter of a pint of Ale, and boyle with three quarters of a pound of sugar, add sixteen egg whites well beaten. Then add this to three pints of boyled cream and stir them well together, then cover it with a Plate and so serve it".

Blackcurrant Jam

4¹/₂ lb/2.05 kg blackcurrants
3 pints/1¹/₂ l water
9 lb/4.1 kg brown sugar

In a wide preserving pan bring to the boil the currants and water, and boil for 20 minutes. Add the brown sugar and bring back to the boil stirring so that the sugar melts. Boil hard for 5 minutes and it should now set when tested.

Warm jam jars. Let the jam cool for a few minutes and then pot up and seal.

Extremely rare seventeenth century brass wine cooler

PRESERVES

> ## The Lord Spencers Cherry water
>
> *Take a pottle of new Sack, four pound of through ripe Cherries stoned, put them into an earthen pot, to which put an ounce of Cinamon, Saffron unbruised one dram, tops of balm, Rosemary or their flowers, of each one handful, let them stand close covered twenty four hours, now and then stirring them: then put them into a cold Still, to which put of beaten Amber two drams, Coriander seed one ounce, Alkerms one dram, and distil it leisurely, and when it is fully distilled put to it twenty grains of Musk. This is an excellent Cordial, good for Faintings and Swoundings, for the Crudities of the Stomach, Winde and swelling of the Bowels, and divers other evil symptomes in the body of men and women.*

The science of distilling was shrouded in mystery and distillers were independent of any controls and operated according to their own individual discretion and sometimes in a manner not conducive to the welfare of the purchasers. This came to the notice of the King's physician, Sir Theodore Mayerne, and he wanted to put distilling on a scientific and sanitary footing. He was a man of high repute and one of the most skilful doctors of his day.

Sir Theodore suggested that there should be a Distiller's Company and Charles I agreed and gave the charter in 1638. Mayerne is named as the Founder. He drew up elaborate instructions for its members which were printed and entitled *The Distillers of London, Compiled and set forth by the Special License and Command of the King's most Excellent Majesty: For the sole use of the Company of Distillers of London. And by them to be duly observed and practised.*

In this book he gives many very precise prescriptions for preparing, distilling, extracting and the making of Rich Spirits, Strong Waters, Aqua Vitae, etc. One recipe says "take strong proof spirit, juniper berries" and then a long list of herbs and roots and "bruise them all, distill them into proof spirit and Dulcifie with white sugar". The result, of course, was something like our present-day liqueurs.

Festivals and holy days were all recognized occasions for feasting and drinking, and ale was the national beverage. Many festivals and social gatherings were held under ecclesiastical auspices and became known as Church Ales, or just Ales. The Whitsun Ales were organized by the Churchwardens, who bought, or were given large amounts of malt which they brewed into beer, which was sold at the feast. Any profits were given to the poor according to the Christian rule that all festivities should be rendered innocent by alms. The church was obviously indulgent in its attitude towards ale which was so much part of everyday life.

Sloe Gin

fat ripe sloes
granulated sugar
gin

Have ready some wine bottles, 75 cl size.

Prick the sloes all over with a darning needle and put into bottles so as to fill them one-third full. Then add 6 oz/175 g sugar to each bottle. Fill up almost to the top with gin, but leave enough headspace for shaking.

Shake the bottles hard every day for 3 weeks so as to extract the juice of the sloes.

Strain through a sieve into a jug and then decant carefully into bottles taking care to leave any sediment behind. It will now be a good purple colour and should be kept for at least 2 years before drinking.

Aubrey describes a Whitsun Ale:

In every parish was a church-house, to which belonged spits, crocks, and other utensils for dressing provisions. Here the housekeepers met. The young people were there too, and had dancing, bowling, shooting at butts etc. The ancients sitting gravely by, and looking on.

Bishop Still wrote the comedy "Gammer Gurton's Needle" with the rollicking song in praise of ale which is one of the first recorded drinking songs.

Back and side go bare, go bare,
Both foot and hand go cold;
But, belly, God send thee good ale enough,
Whether it be new or old.
I cannot eat but little meat,
My stomack is not good;
But sure I think that I can drink
With him that wears a hood.
Though I go bare, take ye no care
I am nothing a-cold.

Ale muller

Wassail cup

> ## To make Paste of Flowers of the Colour of Marble tasting of naturall Flowers
>
> *Take every sort of pleasing flowers, as Violets, Cowslips, Gilly-flowers, Roses or Marygolds, and beat them in a Mortar, each flower by it self with Sugar, till the Sugar become the colour of the flower, then put a little Gum Dragon steept in water into it, and beat it into a perfect paste; and when you have half a dozen colours, every flower will take of his nature, then rowl the Paste therein, and lay one piece upon another, in mingling sort, so rowl your paste in small rowls as bigge and as long as your finger, then cut it off the bignesse of a small nut, overthwart, and so rowl them thin, that you may see a knife through them, so dry them before the fire, till they be dry.*

There must have been considerable distilling as well as brewing, and these distilled spirits were known as Hot Waters.

We know that a ship of 180 tons named the *Mary Rose* sailed over to New England with 120 emigrants and a mixed cargo of meal, shoes, cheese, powder and shot, candles, pewter, soap, nails, wine, vinegar and 250 gallons of Hot Waters. In April 1640 the ship *The Charles* took out 250 passengers and 750 gallons of Hot Waters. This seems a little strange as it was mostly Puritans who were emigrating at this time, and cargo space must have been very valuable.

Shipping in Bristol

Brandy Truffles

6 oz/175 g plain chocolate
6 oz/175 g milk chocolate
1 tablespoon brandy
2 egg yolks
1 dessertspoon double cream
1 oz/25 g butter
Drinking chocolate powder

Break up the chocolate and put in a basin over hot (not boiling) water to melt. When soft remove and stir in the butter, allow to cool. Whisk the egg yolks and cream in another bowl and stir in the brandy; add in the cool chocolate and beat with a wooden spoon. It is important that the mixture is cool enough. Continue beating until it changes texture and becomes like fondant. Quickly roll into balls and roll in drinking chocolate powder.

There is an order passed by the Common Council in Bristol in 1651 that Hot Water houses had increased greatly in number and were being used as tippling houses so that divers persons spent their time and money in drunkenness to the scandal of the city; therefore a new law ordained that sellers of Hot Waters could only sell it to be taken away and not drunk on the premises. If they had seats in their shops or persons were found drinking in them then they would be fined 6 shillings and 8 pence, and the person found drinking would be fined 3 shillings and 4 pence. It is quite clear from this order that Hot Waters were not served in ordinary Inns or Taverns but only in special shops.

Also in Bristol at this time a Night Watch of 17 men were sworn in nightly, and the four ablest guardians of law and order were to enter Inns, Alehouse and Hot Water shops and turn out all found tippling after 10 o'clock at night.

Brandy was first recorded in England in 1657 and it immediately became very popular. The Government saw it as a good source of revenue through Customs duty, and so it soon became a prime cargo for smuggling into Cornish fishing villages on dark nights.

Celia Fiennes describing her journey through Cornwall tells of the very narrow deep lanes where waggons could not pass one another, and then where waggons could not go. She says: "The farther Westward they goe for the wayes grows narrower and narrower on to Lands End". She also describes the packs on the horses that were made like wooden frames and loaded very high and tied with cords so that they could squeeze through the lanes. These could well have carried barrels of brandy.

A Cordial water of Sir Walter Raleigh

Take a Gallon of Strawberries, and put them into a pint of Aqua vitae, let them stand so four or five daies, strain them gently out, and sweeten the water as you please, with a fine Sugar, or else with perfume.

Give me my scallop shell of quiet,
My staff of faith to walk upon,
My scrip of joy, immortal diet,
My bottle of salvation,
My gown of glory, hope's true gage;
And thus I'll take my pilgrimage.

This was written by Sir Walter Raleigh in 1604, and was written while in the Tower at the age of 52.

He was one of the greatest figures in one of the greatest periods of English history and typified the Elizabethan era. He was restless, adventurous and dare-devil all his life being soldier, sailor and explorer. He wrote both beautiful prose and poetry. For 13 years he was imprisoned by James I in the Tower of London, but used his time creatively doing chemical experiments and writing. His poems compare well with any written during the flowering of Elizabethan literature. Having already written and had published his account of his 400 mile journey up the Orinoco river in *The Discovery of Guiana*, he set about writing a *History of the World* for young Prince Henry, who was heir to the throne but died in 1611 leaving Charles to succeed.

Raleigh had had a turbulent relationship with Queen Elizabeth and was a favourite at Court most of the time; there is a line written by him on a window pane:

Fain would I climb, yet fear I to fall.

and under it the Queen wrote;

If thy heart fails thee, climb not at all.

He was released in 1617 at the age of 65 to lead another expedition to Guiana provided he did not come into conflict with the Spaniards, but of course, he did, for attacking Spaniards had become a habit. The Spanish Ambassador demanded his execution as a pirate and James I felt he had to placate Spain.

Written the night before his death and found in his Bible in the Gatehouse at Westminster were the lines:

Even such is time, which takes in trust
Our youth, our joys, and all we have,
And pays us but with age and dust,
Who in the dark and silent grave
When we have wandered all our ways,
Shuts up the story of our days,
And from which earth, and grave and dust,
The Lord shall raise me up, I trust.

Strawberry Liqueur

3 lb/1.35 kg small strawberries
1 lb/450 g sugar
brandy

Prick the strawberries all over with a darning needle and half fill a wide necked jar, or jars. Pour in the sugar and fill the jars with brandy. Cover tightly and stand in a warm place for 6 weeks.

Strain the liquid into small bottles and cork securely and store.

Walter Raleigh and son

PRESERVES

To Pickle Cucumbers

Put them in an Earthen Vessel, lay first a Lay of Salt, and Dill, then a Lay of Cucumbers, and so till they be all Layed, put in some Mace und whole Pepper, and some Fennel-seed according to direction, then fill it up with Beer Vinegar, and a clean board, and a stone upon it, to keep them within the Pickle, and so keep them close covered, and if the Viaegar is black change them into fresh.

The King and Queen travelled in the summertime and went on a "progress". They set off with most of the Court in attendance soon after Easter and stayed in various royal residences in the country. They stayed a few weeks in each and travelling in this way were seen by more of their subjects. While going from one residence to another they would call in and see the local nobility causing a great stir and a feverish activity of preparation. They called on the Spencers and spent a day at Althorpe and the household accounts show that over £800 was paid out in one week.

It was thought necessary to improve the Great Chamber for the occasion and so new matting, gilt leather hangings and gilt chairs and stools were bought.

Special kitchen ranges were installed, and it took one man 7 days and nights to make racks for roasting the meat. Another spent 4 days and 1 night carrying water to the kitchen and the dog-kennel yard and 3 days cleansing the courts for which he was paid 5 shillings and 4 pence.

Others were paid for bringing cakes from Shropshire and for fetching borrowed plate from Holdenby. It took 3 women 2 days to pluck all the poultry. One thousand eggs were bought for the household.

Sundry expenses included £2 for music, and "ten yards of Kersey for my Lady". The Wine bill for the banquet came to £76. Other things needed were:

500 lbs of butter at 5 pence a pound

125 quarts of cream

13 veals

8 doz lemons of the 1st sort

2 great pikes

39 dozen larks

33 turkeys

26 pigs

8 doz lemons of the 2nd sort

23 couple rabbits

also "parsenippes, carrootes, cabbidges, herbes, hartichoakes and cowcumbers".

Neighbouring gentry rallied round to help sending duckling, quail, pheasants and partridges. One servant had to be tipped for bringing and taking back 18 spits, and Lord Brookes' man had to be paid his "fee for stags".

Cucumber Pickle

2 lb/900 g cucumber
2 large onions
1 red and 1 green pepper
salt
3/4 pint/425 ml cider vinegar
8 oz/225 g sugar
2 tablespoons mustard seed
1 teaspoon ground ginger

Slice up the fruit and put in a large bowl and sprinkle liberally with salt; leave overnight. Drain and rinse and drain again well.

Put vinegar, sugar and ginger in a large pan. Bring to the boil and simmer for 5 minutes, then put into warm jars and seal.

One can imagine all the organization beforehand, the hustle and bustle, and the exhaustion after the Royal guests had departed, and the wonderful topic provided for endless conversation and anecdote to last through the coming winter months.

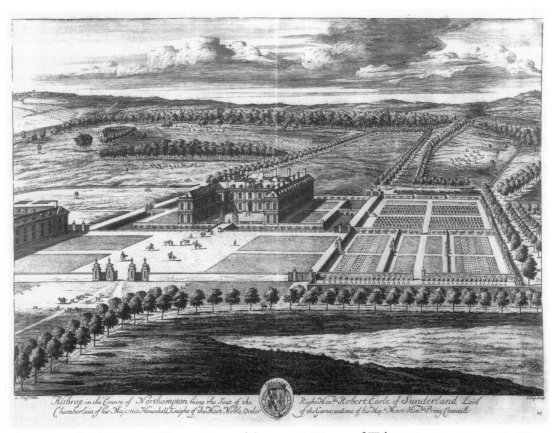

The Spencer family home at Althorp – home of the present Princess of Wales (Bodleian, Douce Prints a 24, plate 27)

Index of recipes

Index